WADSWORTH PHILOSC

c/

ON

PASCAL

Douglas Groothuis
Denver Seminary

Australia • Canada • Mexico • Singapore • Spain • United Kingdom • United States

For more information about our
products, contact us at:
Thomson Learning Academic
Resource Center
1-800-423-0563

For permission to use material from
this text, contact us by:
Phone: 1-800-730-2214
Fax: 1-800-731-2215
Web: www.thomsonrights.com

Asia
Thomson Learning
5 Shenton Way #01-01
UIC Building
Singapore 068808

Australia
Nelson Thomson Learning
102 Dodds Street
South Street
South Melbourne, Victoria 3205
Australia

Canada
Nelson Thomson Learning
1120 Birchmount Road
Toronto, Ontario M1K 5G4
Canada

Europe/Middle East/South Africa
Thomson Learning
High Holborn House
50-51 Bedford Row
London WC1R 4LR
United Kingdom

Latin America
Thomson Learning
Seneca, 53
Colonia Polanco
11560 Mexico D.F.
Mexico

Spain
Paraninfo Thomson Learning
Calle/Magallanes, 25
28015 Madrid, Spain

Contents

Preface

A small book on a great thinker is a tall order. In Blaise Pascal one discovers a brilliant intellect who combined scientific and philosophical acumen with a lucid and memorable style. Pascal addressed matters of ultimate concern with great urgency, cogency, and even humor. Although much of his work was left unfinished at this early death in 1662, the literary remnants have charmed, puzzled, inspired and infuriated scores of readers over the centuries on a wide variety of subjects.

Despite his notability and ongoing popularity, some have taken Pascal to be an irrationalist who pitted faith against reason, a misanthrope who deemed humans to be vile and worthless, and one who in later life abandoned and condemned the scientific pursuits in which he once excelled. The truth, however, is much more complex—and much more interesting. I hope this small volume will stimulate many readers to join the ongoing conversation with this French polymath as he muses over God, the paradoxes of the human condition, the powers and limits of science, morality, the meaning of life, and spirituality.

One important note on documentation. All quotes from *Pensées* (or *Thoughts*) are referenced by two numbers in parentheses after the quote. The first number refers to the newer Lafuma enumeration of Pascal's fragments used in the Penguin edition (1966), translated by Alban Krailsheimer. The second number refers to the older Brunschvicg ordering of fragments used in The Harvard Classics and Great Books editions.

My thanks to Dr. Daniel Kolak, editor of the Wadsworth Philosophers Series, for his encouragement in the writing of this book. I also thank Dr. Louis Pojman for connecting me with Wadsworth. I dedicate this book to my inestimable wife, Rebecca Merrill Groothuis, whose inspiration and assistance were indispensable.

1

Blaise Pascal: Known and Unknown

Scientist, inventor, philosopher, mystic, and theologian, Blaise Pascal (1623-1662) is more often quoted than understood. Strangely, he is both well-known and largely unknown. Although he may appear in books of famous quotations more frequently than other philosophers, histories of philosophy often omit any reference to him; and anthologies typically feature only his famous wager fragment, in which he recommends betting on God's existence in view of the costs and benefits involved. Consequently, some of the most invigorating and vexing of his ideas are hidden. Many know that the computer language "Pascal" is named after the man who invented the first calculator, but few know of his revolutionary philosophy of science, his other scientific achievements, his probing reflections on ethics, or his piercing reflections on the enigmas of human nature.

The Heart of Pascal

Pascal's most enduring work, *Pensées*, is a collection of posthumously published fragments that Pascal had intended to become part of a book defending the Christian religion. These fragments have been assembled in several arrangements, none of which provides a clearly linear or systematic development of his viewpoints. Therefore, some approach Pascal with a smorgasbord sensibility. Various memorable and arresting aphorisms and epigrams are snatched up, pondered, and even savored, but often at the expense of knowing what they mean or how they fit into the larger puzzle of Pascal's philosophy.

1

Consider this curiously luminous sentence: "The heart has its reasons of which reason knows nothing: we know this in countless ways" (432/277). Scores have been entranced by the poetic and paradoxical ring of this sentence. But what did Pascal mean by it?

Some have taken "reasons of the heart" to refer to an irrational, emotional, or otherwise arbitrary preference or orientation. If so, so much the worse for Pascal. If "reasons of the heart" are bereft of rational justification they cannot be subject to logical evaluation. They would be either nonrational (such as a sneeze or wheeze) or irrational (such as believing in unicorns). This is no position for a *philosopher* to take. Or did Pascal have something very different in mind—something more subtle, profound, and complex? Could the same man who amazed all of Europe with his mathematical and scientific abilities disengage the head entirely for "reasons of the heart"?

Many think that Pascal was a fideist: one who divorces faith and reason and finds no rational support for religious belief. One might claim that in matters of mathematical calculation and scientific experimentation Pascal employed reason and observation, but in the realm of religion he took another course. Some of his statements—taken by themselves—can indeed be read in this way. "It is the heart which perceives God and not the reason. That is what faith is: God perceived by the heart, not by reason" (424/278).

For Pascal, belief in God, the church, and the Christian Scriptures meant far more than assenting to the conclusion of a complex argument; faith involved submitting the core of one's being to a supernatural being who calls one into a transformational encounter and an ongoing engagement. On the other hand, Pascal, in the last few years of his life, proposed to write a reasoned defense of the Christian religion (*Apology for the Christian Religion*), which would win over the skeptics and unbelievers of his day to Christian commitment. One of the fragments from that intended work was so bold as to claim that, "One of the ways in which the damned will be confounded is that they will see themselves condemned by their own reason, by which they claimed to condemn the Christian religion" (175/563).

When Pascal laid out the strategy for this defense of Christianity, he did not dispense with reason as a tool for commending faith; he did not lay aside his prodigious intellectual skills by abandoning rational argumentation. Consider his program for his proposed apology.

Order. Men despise religion. They hate it and are afraid it may be true. The cure for this is to show that religion is not contrary

2

to reason, but worthy of reverence and respect. Next make it attractive, make good men wish it were true, and then show that it is. Worthy of reverence because it really understands human nature. Attractive because it promises true good (12/187).

Some of Pascal's most memorable and oft-repeated sayings concern the strangeness and wonder of the human condition. But these were never offered as snippets of wisdom without purpose. They fit integrally into Pascal's claim that Christianity is "worthy of reverence because it really understands human nature." The apologist applied his considerable philosophical and rhetorical skills to that end, relying on the biblical account of human nature as his guide.

Was Pascal an Existentialist?

Pascal's emphasis on the lived experience of Christian faith and its pertinence to the individual believer has inclined some to classify him as an early existentialist, even as a precursor to Søren Kierkegaard (1813-1855), the prolific Danish, Christian writer and "father of existentialism." Although we do find some existentialist themes in Pascal—the vexing nature of existence, distrust of impersonal and abstract systems of thought, and a rejection of traditional proofs for God's existence—he is better studied in his own right than pigeonholed by a term only coined in the mid-twentieth century to describe quite different kinds of thinkers. None of the existentialists, for example, were accomplished scientists (many pitted their philosophies against science) nor did any develop a philosophy of science that was theologically informed. Pascal regarded reason more highly than most existentialists, although he highlighted the effects of sin on human thought. In any event, we should let Pascal speak in his own genuine voice, whatever loose affinities he may have had with existentialism.[1]

Was Pascal a Philosopher?

Pascal's essentially religious or theological outlook has led some commentators to exclude his work from that of philosophy proper or to judge his work as poor philosophy. Some have argued that the title "philosopher" should be used to designate only those who speculate widely and systematically, and who appeal only to human reason apart

3

Blaise Pascal: Known and Unknown

from any consideration of divine revelation or awareness of a religious mission. But this prejudices the case against the entire stream of influential religious thinkers who have pondered reality deeply and logically in light of their spiritual convictions. It also prejudges the case against less systematic and nonreligious thinkers such as Friedrich Nietzsche (1844-1900). Any definition of philosophy that excludes in principle Augustine, Anselm or Martin Buber—passionate religious believers as well as earnest, vigilant thinkers—is surely defective and should be discarded swiftly.

Nevertheless, Pascal did not approach philosophy as a vocation. His fame in his day came from his genius as mathematician, physicist, and inventor. His religious writings concerned theological disputes and apologetics (the defense of the Christian faith as objectively true and rationally credible). Nevertheless, there was no little philosophizing in Pascal's writings, especially throughout *Pensées*. Although he did not develop a systematic philosophy, it is unfair to rank him as merely a minor philosopher. His thoughts are too large.

Another strike against considering Pascal as a genuine philosopher is the fact that he left us no final, systematic philosophical statement. Instead, we must reconstruct his views from a set of published polemical letters on theology, personal correspondence, several works on science, some scattered essays, and *Pensées*. Although many have wondered what sort of finished work of philosophy Pascal would have left us, the lack of a well-organized, detailed philosophy affords the earnest reader some advantages.

As they stand, the many absorbing and arresting fragments of the *Pensées* furnish us with raw materials for an intellectual adventure concerning our uneasy place in an often perplexing cosmos and culture. Unlike the more methodical philosophers, such as Descartes, Pascal in many cases does not finish a line of thought for us. Instead he initiates an intellectual pursuit that we are left to follow-up on—or ignore. Some of the fragments of *Pensées* are not arguments at all, but evocative parables meant to trigger a new kind of awareness.

> Imagine a number of men in chains, all under sentence of death, some of whom are each day butchered in the sight of the others; those remaining see their own condition in that of their fellows, and looking at each other with grief and despair await their turn. This is an image of the human condition (434/199).

Discerning the meaning of these passages in light of Pascal's other writings requires an active and imaginative engagement of one's philosophical prowess. A pattern can be found; and although the search is not simple, it is, I believe, supremely rewarding.

Pascal entered deeply into human experience and left little that is distinctly human unobserved or unexamined. That is one reason why we often find ourselves in his ruminations. He did not paint the human condition in lifeless, predictable or untroubled hues. His portrait was disturbingly lifelike and vividly articulated across the full spectrum of humanity. There is a poetic and authentic quality to much of his writing; it is not detached, speculative, or pedantic.

The Wager on God

It is probably Pascal's famed wager argument that has done the most to obscure and overshadow other crucial aspects of his reflections and provocations. Those who know little about Pascal have usually heard of his claim that one would be better off if one were to believe in God even if God does not exist than if one were to disbelieve in God if God does exist. Pascal's essential insight is found in a shorter fragment from *Pensées*: "I should be much more afraid of being mistaken and then finding out that Christianity is true than of being mistaken in believing it to be true" (387/241).

This fascinating argument, closely connected to his investigation of probability theory, has perhaps received more philosophical attention in recent years than any other aspect of Pascal's writings. Yet these discussions are usually divorced from key elements of Pascal's overall approach to religious belief, thus giving a distorted picture of the role the wager plays in Pascal's thought. Until quite recently, most academic articles ridiculed the wager. However, contemporary philosophers have been finding more charitable and credible ways to defend it or a revised form of it. It is a puzzling, easily misunderstood, but intellectually fertile piece of philosophical reasoning.

Caught Between Two Ages

One fruitful way to disclose the meaning, significance, and ongoing importance of Pascal—and to move beyond ignorance and clichés—is to conceive of him as a thinker caught between two ages. He was one of the first modern Christian intellectuals who was neither

5

medieval nor a figure of the Enlightenment.[2] Despite his strong sympathies with Jansenism, an Augustianian reform movement within Catholicism, he was a loyal son of the church and did not want to adjust its theology to the spirit of the times. Yet because he lived after the Reformation—an event that dislodged the papacy's medieval hegemony over Europe and divided Christendom theologically and politically—he could not assume or address a unified body of Christians. Because of his bitter disputes with the Jesuits, recorded in his *Provincial Letters (Lettres Provinciales)* he was sometimes accused of having sympathies with Protestants, a claim he vehemently and rightly denied.

It was Pascal—the physicist, mathematician, inventor, and philosopher of science—who also helped instigate the scientific revolution, which would begin to challenge many of the received truths of Christian Europe. Descartes reconceptualized nature as a grand mechanism, thus driving a wedge between mind (or spirit) and body, and bringing into question the traditional accounts of nature and its relationship to its Creator. If the universe is a vast machine, could it run on its own? How could God relate to it? Pascal endorsed much of the new Cartesian picture, but, unlike his fellow Frenchman, he was as passionate about his religious convictions as he was about his scientific pursuits. In later life, Pascal would warn of "those who probe science too deeply. Descartes" (553/76; see also 22/367).

Besides charting a new, but theistic, conception of nature with respect to science, Pascal also broke from the medieval conception of natural theology, by which philosophers attempted to prove logically God's existence through premises derived from the natural world. Pascal dispensed with these theistic arguments for several reasons, although he did advance another kind of philosophical apologetic in *Pensées*.

Before we outline the basic lineaments of Pascal's philosophy and move beyond the many stereotypes based on ignorance, we need to learn more about this remarkable man and his fascinating times.

---

[1] See Leszek Kolakowski, *God Owes us Nothing: A Brief Remark on Pascal's Religion and on the Spirit of Jansenism* (Chicago: University of Chicago Press, 1995), 187-190.
[2] See Edward T. Oakes, "Pascal: The First Modern Christian," *First Things* (August/September 1999), 41-48.

2

A Short Life of Pascal

Blaise Pascal, the son of a French governmental official and lawyer, was born into a century of philosophical and scientific genius in Europe, often called (not without warrant) the Age of Reason. At the time of Pascal's birth on June 19, 1623, in Clermont (now Clermont-Ferrard) in Auvergne, France, René Descartes (1596-1650) was in his mid-twenties. Descartes was then working on his revolutionary philosophical treatise, *The Rules for the Direction of the Mind*, while traveling through Europe in order, he claimed, to discover truth.

Scientist Isaac Newton (1642-1727) and philosopher Gottfried Leibniz (1646-1716) would be born not long after and would go on to develop several of Pascal's mathematical insights. Galileo Galilei (1564-1642) began writing his seminal *Dialogue on the Two Principle World Systems* the year of Pascal's birth. The seventeenth century was also that of the Jewish philosopher Baruch Spinoza (1632-1677), who would take the rationalistic Cartesian method of philosophizing to the extreme in his deductive and geometrically-oriented works. Voltaire (1694-1778), the French skeptic and a critic of Pascal, was born near the end of this century of intellectual discovery and controversy.

Pascal made his mark on this great century—and beyond it to our day—although he never held an academic or governmental position, never went to college, and was in ill health most of his short life. His devout mother died in 1626, leaving young Blaise and his two living sisters—one younger (Jacqueline) and one older (Gilberte)—to be raised by his father Étienne. (The first daughter had died in infancy). Étienne was a Latinist, an excellent mathematician, and had a keen interest in natural science. Étienne was, and wanted his son to become,

7

what was known in seventeenth-century France as an "*honnête homme*" (honest man): an aristocratic man of culture, civility, self-sufficiency, and discernment.

How to Educate a Genius

After his wife's death, the elder Pascal took an early retirement and moved his family to Paris in 1631, in order to participate in its exemplary intellectual culture. Étienne broke with tradition and educated his sickly and high-strung son entirely at home, as he did his daughters. In our terms, he was a stay-at-home dad and a home-schooler. His teaching emphasized problem-solving, rather than offering material to memorize. This instilled in Blaise a sense of curiosity and adventure in learning. Going against the educational tradition of his day, Étienne began Blaise's education exclusively with Latin and Greek, and postponed his instruction in mathematics.

However, Étienne did speak briefly to the inquisitive Blaise about the basic nature of mathematics. This was enough to shift the youngster's mind into high gear. Sister Gilberte recounts that her father discovered his untaught twelve-year-old son working out Euclid's geometry to the thirty-second proposition. Whether strictly factual or a bit exaggerated, the account illustrates Pascal's prodigious and precocious abilities.

His father's method of instruction, coupled with his own genius, fostered in Pascal a great confidence in his abilities, as well as an intellectual bravado. This cockiness, while serving him well in science, would need to be tamed—even crucified—in his later religious endeavors, which become quite ascetic near the end of his life.

After Blaise's display of mathematical aptitude, Étienne wisely lifted the ban and formally acquainted his son with Euclid. Not long after, father and son began to attend the prestigious weekly mathematical meetings of Father Marin Mersenne (1588-1648), a friend of Descartes. French high society was quite taken with natural philosophy (which comprised what we now call science and philosophy), and some of its celebrities were superb mathematicians. While contemporary American culture celebrates entrepreneurs and entertainers, the life of the mind was central to Parisians in Pascal's youth. Young Blaise thrived in this heady and intellectually challenging ambiance and elicited no little praise—and probably some envy—for his advanced and unusual abilities.

The Maturing Scientist

In 1637, after raising the ire of the powerful Cardinal Richelieu in a governmental dispute, Étienne fled Paris and returned to Auvergne for a time. Shortly thereafter, Blaise's younger sister Jacqueline, who was talented in poetry and acting, performed before Richelieu in such a winsome manner as to win back some favor for the Pascal family. Étienne was then commissioned to collect taxes at Rouen, a city recently troubled by civil strife over taxation. The recent unrest made being a civil servant a tough assignment. It was there that Pascal, while still a teenager, published in 1640 his first major work, *Essay on Conic Sections* (*Essai pour les coniques*), a small treatise on projective geometry. In 1642, Pascal invented and supervised the arduous construction of the first adding machine for the purpose of helping his father with the onerous task of calculating taxes. Upon the Pascal family's return to Paris in 1648, Pascal again accompanied his father to some of the weekly meetings of noteworthy scientists, which they had previously frequented.

From about 1646 until 1651 Pascal designed ground-breaking experiments related to atmospheric pressures and the existence of vacuums and engaged in other significant scientific pursuits. On September 23 and 24, 1647, Pascal was visited by the illustrious Descartes, who admired Pascal's adding machine, but disputed his claim that nature did not necessarily abhor a vacuum. Descartes may also have made medical recommendations to the ailing younger scientist. This was likely their only personal encounter, but Descartes's reasoning on a variety of subjects could not be ignored by Pascal—or any other thinking European.

Spiritual Discovery: First Conversion

An injured leg initiated a spiritual turning point for the Pascal family in 1646. After wounding his thigh from slipping on ice, Étienne was attended for three months by two young brothers who were amateur bone-setters. More importantly, they were influenced by Jansenism, an Augustinian reform movement within Catholicism, and had been converted from wild lives of dueling and womanizing. As devout Catholics, the Pascals were impressed by the sincerity, earnestness, and practicality of the young men's faith. That faith emphasized a deep prayer life, a cognizance of human sinfulness, and

9

the need for God's grace in salvation; it also rejected a mechanical reliance on religious ceremony or human merit as a means of salvation. This spirituality particularly influenced Blaise and Jacqueline. She eventually became a Jansenist nun at the abbey of Port-Royal des Champes, a country outpost of the Port-Royal abbey just outside of Paris.

These men gave Pascal the spiritual works of Cornelius Jansen, the father of Jansenism; Saint-Cyran, the spiritual director of Port-Royal; and Antoine Arnauld, a philosopher and theologian. These writings all affected him deeply. Little did Pascal know that these humble and unassuming servants had introduced him to a movement that eventually would enlist his aid in their bitter and dangerous controversies with the Jesuit establishment and even with the pope himself. This exposure to a more serious faith lead to what many call Pascal's "first conversion," although he was not irreligious before this time.

Theological Controversies and Sickness

By 1647, Pascal's physical condition became increasingly sickly. Jacqueline writes of his terrible headaches, indigestion, and inability to swallow cool liquids. His medicine had to be taken heated, drop by drop. "All this resulted in a condition painful in the extreme, though my brother never uttered a word of complaint."[1] After a serious illness in the summer 1647, his physicians recommended that he avoid undue stress and cease his concentrated intellectual endeavors. Instead, the driven scientist and inventor should seek some diversion. Reluctantly, he acquiesced, "believing himself to be obliged to do everything possible to restore his health and imagining that upright diversions could not but help promote it. So it was that he turned for solace to the world."[2] For Pascal, this meant tennis, hunting, dancing, theatre, and especially gambling. Some of the most poignant and true-to-life fragments in the *Pensées* take up the follies and deceptions of diversion. "If our condition were truly happy we should not need to divert ourselves from thinking about it" (70/165).

These activities did not have the desired long-term physical effects, although Pascal did socialize with some vigor. He began to partake of Paris's high society with several less-than-pious friends, who enjoyed gambling, socializing, and worldly enterprise. These characters sometimes appear as a focus of concern in the *Pensées*. One companion, Damien Mitten, is mentioned by name several times.

Pascal initially got on quite well in these environs and was the darling of the royal court, given his penchant for enchanting conversation, a prized art in that day. Pascal was hardly dissolute during this time; he engaged in much scientific endeavor (despite the doctor's warnings against it) and began to attend the abbey of Port-Royal near Paris with Jacqueline to hear Jansenist preaching. Jacqueline had resolved to become a nun, but her father's opposition prohibited this until his death in 1651.

The elder Pascal's death was deeply felt by Blaise, as it was by the rest of his close-knit family. It occasioned a long, serious and theologically rich letter by Pascal in which he sounds some themes which play a major role in his later philosophical and theological writings. "We should seek consolation in our ills, not in ourselves, not in men, not in any thing that is created; but in God." The senior Pascal's death, his son counsels, should not be regarded as the result of chance, "but as a result indispensable, inevitable, just, holy, useful to the good of the Church, and to the exaltation of the name and the greatness of God, of a decree of his providence conceived from all eternity."[3]

Pascal claims that "it is certain that Socrates and Seneca have nothing consolatory on such an occasion as this," since they take death to be natural and not due to sin. "There is no consolation, but in truth alone."[4] The crux for Pascal is this: "Without Jesus Christ [death] is horrible, detestable, the horror of nature. In Jesus Christ it is altogether different; it is benignant, holy, the joy of the faithful."[5] Despite the letter's sobriety, Pascal's full dedication to Christianity would not come until another sorrow brought his spiritual devotion into question. Echoing Augustine, Pascal wrote:

God has created man with two loves, the one for God, the other for himself; but with this law, that the love for God shall be infinite, that is, without any other limits than God himself; and that the love of self shall be finite and relating to God.[6]

Although he had initially agreed with Jacqueline's decision to become a nun at Port-Royal, Pascal demurred after his father's death, thus causing a painful rift with his beloved and devout sister. Pascal may have objected because he feared the loss of his sister's company and the loss of finances that would result from her donating her share of their inheritance to Port-Royal as her dowry.

Nevertheless, Jacqueline was resolute. After a meeting with the formidable head of the abbey, Mère Angélique Arnauld, Pascal relented. He attended the ceremony of his sister's final vows as a novice in May of 1652, but not with rejoicing.

Despite Pascal's popularity and growing renown in French high society, the experiment with worldliness as a cure for illness was failing. He was not a well man, despite his notoriety. Pascal was restless and lacked the financial security he desired. He then began to visit Jacqueline often, speaking to her through the grill, as was required of sequestered nuns at Port-Royal des Champes. After one of his visits, Jacqueline wrote to her sister that her brother was weary with the world; however, he was not yet ready to turn wholeheartedly to God, which distressed her considerably.

Fire: The Second Conversion

The next pivotal event in Pascal's life was only unveiled after his death in 1662. To our knowledge, he did not mention it to a soul. Among Pascal's personal effects was found a jacket that contained a piece of paper and a parchment sown into the inner lining. Apparently, Pascal had transferred these materials to every new jacket he acquired until his death. He may have carried it with him constantly next to his heart. Inscribed on the paper was a terse and poetic account of an experience dated November 23, 1654. The paper seems to be the original record of the event. The manner of writing suggests it was written quickly in order to record accurately the significance of what is described. The parchment appears to be a copy of the original account, with some additions and variations. I will quote from the parchment. This account, referred to as "The Memorial," is often described as "the night of fire." After introducing the religious significance of the day, Pascal writes,

From about half past ten in the evening until half past mid-night.

Fire

'God of Abraham, God of Isaac, God of Jacob,' not of
philosophers and scholars.
Certainty, certainty, heartfelt joy, peace
God of Jesus Christ
God of Jesus Christ
My God and your God.

'Thy God shall be my God.'
The world forgotten, and everything except God
He can only be found by the ways taught in the Gospels
Greatness of the human soul.
'Oh righteous Father, the world had not known thee, but I
have known thee'
       Joy, joy, joy, tears of joy.
I have cut myself off from him
They have forsaken me, the foundation of living waters.
'My God wilt thou forsake me?'

Let me not be cut off from him for ever!
'And this is life eternal, that they might know thee, the only
true God, and Jesus Christ whom thou has sent'
Jesus Christ.
Jesus Christ.
I have cut myself off from him, shunned him, denied him,
crucified him.
Let me never be cut off from him!
He can only be kept by the ways taught in the Gospel.
Sweet and total renunciation.
Total submission to Jesus Christ and my director
Everlasting joy in return for one day's effort on earth.
I will not forget thy word. Amen.[7]

    Pascal employs staccato statements, several of which are repeated, interspersed with biblical quotations. The now famous Memorial was not meant for publication. It bears testimony to a transformational event in which Pascal apprehends the holy and joyous fire of the living God, not the cold abstractions of mere philosophy or scholarship. The revelation also discloses both Pascal's sense of estrangement and his reconciliation to God—as well as his passion to "never be cut off from him." A new consecration emerges, a "total submission to Jesus Christ" and a pledge to honor Scripture ("I will not forget thy word," taken from Psalm 119).
    The statement concerning "submission to...my director," is not included in the paper statement, was probably added to the parchment version. Its significance should not be missed. Pascal had been a proud, ambitious, and celebrated man as well as an acclaimed prodigy and genius. He had initially opposed Jacqueline's admission to Port-Royal des Champes. Now he himself would go on retreats and submit to a spiritual director at Port-Royal, although he would not become a full-

fledged solitary there. Pascal's "fire" experience may have been behind his pithy exclamation, "What a long way it is between knowing God and loving him" (377/280).

Pascal's "second conversion" would not spell the end of his scientific endeavors. However, scientific discovery would no longer be his ruling passion. He resolved to champion the cause of the Jansenists against their Jesuit antagonists in a series of letters written under a pseudonym. *The Provincial Letters* became a classic of polemical literature and helped turn public acceptance toward the reform movement, although it was a short-lived victory.

More importantly, the recreated Pascal began to compose a defense of the Christian religion, aimed at the kind of freethinkers and other unbelievers with whom he had associated during the worldly period. But he either gave up on the project or, more probably, died before it could be completed. Only in the last five years of his life did he begin to write down his thoughts on the subject, lest he forget them due to his declining health. What remains of these notes to himself, the *Pensées*, has been eminently influential since its posthumous publication in 1669.

Final Suffering, Extremity, and Service

Eventually, Pascal withdrew from the controversy over Port-Royal and Jansenism, but not without a fight. The tide had turned against them, and there was little left to do. Henceforth, Pascal pursued a life of voluntary poverty, prayer, and service to the poor. He refused to use servants or eat seasoned foods, gave away most of his possessions, including all of his books except the Bible, St. Augustine's *Confessions*, and a few others. His asceticism could be extreme. He would secretly push a spiked iron belt into his flesh when he found himself enjoying conversations. He scolded his sister Gilberte for caressing her small children and denounced the idea that her fifteen-year-old daughter should be married to a wealthy suitor, since marriage was entirely unworthy of a spiritual person. Pascal prevailed; she never married. He wrote that no one should love him or be attached to him. Despite this religious zeal, Pascal would be hard-pressed to find biblical support for his extremism.

But Pascal did not renounce helping others. He took the poor into his home. In the last year of his life he designed the first omnibus, or public transport, to serve the poor of Paris, and established a company to oversee its execution. This was the same man who a few years earlier dashed about Paris in his fine carriage. He prepared his will with ample provision for the poor. He wrote, "I love poverty because he [Jesus Christ] loved it. I love wealth because it affords me the means of helping the needy. I keep faith with everyone" (931/550).

Despite his controversies with the Catholic authorities, Pascal left this world with the blessings of the church. He died shortly after receiving extreme unction and taking the Eucharist with tears. His last words on August 19, 1662, were, "May God never forsake me." He was thirty-nine years and two months old. An autopsy revealed a profoundly diseased body. According to his niece, who gave a surprisingly detailed report, his stomach had withered away and his intestines were gangrenous. There were several abnormalities of the brain as well.

"Man," Pascal wrote, is "only a reed, the weakest in nature, but he is a thinking reed" (200/347). Pascal himself was a striking example of this paradoxical identity: weak body, strong mind, and—especially toward the end—a large heart for the poor of Paris.

Pascal's funeral was attended by a throng of people of all stripes—family members, friends, scientific colleagues, worldly companions, writers, converts, and, hiding in the back, several members of Port-Royal, who risked arrest by attending. Most of the rear of the church was packed with the sort of poor folks for whom Pascal had offered service in his final years of suffering.

---

[1] Marvin R. O'Connell, *Blaise Pascal: Reasons of the Heart* (Grand Rapids, MI: William B. Eerdmans Publishing, 1997), 83.
[2] Ibid., 84.
[3] Blaise Pascal, *"Lettre sur la mort de son pere,"* *Thoughts, Letters, Minor Works*, ed. Charles W. Eliot. The Harvard Classics, vol. 48 (New York: P.F. Collier and Son Company, 1910), 336.
[4] Ibid., 337.
[5] Ibid., 338.
[6] Ibid., 341.
[7] Blaise Pascal, *Pensées*, ed. A. Krailsheimer (New York: Penguin, 1966), 309-310.

3

Scientist and Philosopher of Science

Pascal's renown in his day came chiefly through his achievements in science and mathematics. He is now better known for his comment popularly referred to as "the God-shaped vacuum" in each of us, than he is recognized as the defender of the existence of the vacuum in nature. He is known more for his "wager" argument than for his formal theorizing about probabilities. Nevertheless, a survey of Pascal's scientific endeavors and his reflections on science sheds light on the relationship of science and religion and illuminates other aspects of his thought. Although Pascal became increasingly devoted to religion in later life, he did not disparage scientific pursuits if they were practiced in the proper spirit.

Pascal's instruction by his father cultivated independent investigation and discovery. In 1640, Pascal got his first taste of notoriety when his *Essay on Conic Sections* (*Essai pour les coniques*) was published. This was an illustrated treatise that treated conics as plane sections through a circular cone and expanded the innovative projective geometry of Gérard Desargues (1593-1662). By this time, Pascal had also proposed a theory that came to be called Pascal's Theorem of the Mystic Hexagon.[1] Despite the appreciation he received from many scientists at the time, Pascal was snubbed by Descartes, who became something of an intellectual rival.[2]

The Calculator and Probability Theory

To help his father assess taxes, Pascal designed and built the first functional calculator. Today when digital devices are everywhere, we should escape our historical myopia and ponder the impact of a calculating machine on Pascal's contemporaries. Pascal designed a *machine* to perform functions previously calculated only by the *mind*. Others had tried to engineer such a category-bending device, but Pascal succeeded as no one had before.

He formulated the notion of the calculating machine in 1642. Two years later a craftsman produced the first working model under Pascal's direction. Despite its cumbersome nature, this prototype of the computer added, subtracted, multiplied, and divided numbers with as many as eight digits. Pascal worked ardently for approximately a decade on perfecting the machine, after which he devised an advertising strategy to market the labor-saving device. Although fifty such proto-computers were built, Pascal was not destined to be a seventeenth-century Bill Gates. Expense and difficulties in production limited its popularity, much to Pascal's distress. Eight specimens of Pascal's machine remain today, one owned by IBM, appropriately enough.[3] In honor of his achievement, one of the earliest computer languages was named "Pascal" in 1971.

Pascal's work on probability theory began when a friend who gambled challenged Pascal to calculate the equitable portion of stakes to be rewarded to players in a game of chance that was interrupted before its completion. Pascal then corresponded on the matter with Pierre de Fermat, the well-known mathematician, in 1654. The resulting *Treatise on the Arithmetical Triangle* (*Traité du Triangle arithmétique*) contained important work in combinatorial analysis. The question of probable outcomes with respect to high stakes would also factor into Pascal's famous wager argument from the *Pensées* (418/233; see also 577/234).

The Existence of the Vacuum

Pascal's greatest scientific accomplishment was his work on the vacuum. These reflections were also pivotal in the development of an empirically-based scientific method. Although it is assumed today that scientific nature should be grounded in repeatable observation as much as possible, this was disputed in Pascal's day. Cosmology was dominated by two very different and antithetical views, both of which, nevertheless, were united in their denial of the existence of a vacuum. There was the Aristotelian and later medieval notion that nature was a hierarchical plenum or continuum devoid of any gaps. This was

17

sometimes called "the great chain of being." In this qualitatively oriented cosmology, substances were thought to possess "occult qualities" or forms: heaviness makes lead fall faster than a feather, whose defining quality is lightness. Wood burns because it has the form of being combustible, and so on.

A second reason invoked in favor of the maxim that "nature abhors a vacuum" was the newer and revolutionary theory of Descartes. Instead of a qualitative concept of nature, Descartes attempted to explain matter (which he defined as extension) in strictly quantitative terms. Mathematics and mechanics could explain physical phenomena in all its forms without appeal to qualitative terms. This view would simplify and unify the sciences according to physical laws deductively derived according to *a priori* principles apart from experimentation. Matter was interchangeable with the geometrical points, or space, in which it is located. Matter, understood as extension, is identical with physical space. Therefore, the idea of empty space (or a vacuum) is a contradiction in terms within the Cartesian system.

Experimentation, for Descartes, might serve to illustrate a rational truth or theory, but it did not have the vital role of producing newly discovered truth about nature. Further, Descartes' view deemed a vacuum impossible. If there is nothing between two bodies, they must in fact be in contact; there can be no gap between instances of extension. If a tube contained a vacuum, Descartes postulated, its sides would collapse upon each other. Since experiments concerning the vacuum did not yield this result, there is no vacuum. In this sense, he did appeal to empirical factors, but only in a negative way.

Pascal, however, was not convinced by either argument against the vacuum. The traditional "plenists" (who abhorred the vacuum) did not impress him. Pascal clearly distinguished between the authority delivered by religion and the need for independent, empirical observation in matters not directly addressed in sacred writ or church tradition. In October of 1646, the year of his "first conversion," Pascal repeated the barometric experiments of Evangelista Torricelli (1608-47), a disciple of Galileo, which had caused quite a stir among natural philosophers. By inverting a long glass tube filled with mercury in a bowl of mercury, he noticed that the mercury in the tube dropped down until it was about 76 cm above the level in the bowl. The purpose of the experiment was to confirm Galileo's suspicions about the role of the atmosphere in limiting the height to which a pump could lift water. It also suggested that when the mercury dropped, the space remaining at the end of the tube must be a vacuum. This, of course, struck an experimental blow against the vacuum haters.

In 1647, Pascal published the results of his barometric experiments in *New Experiments Concerning the Vacuum (Expériences nouvelles touchant le vide)*. After a series of detailed experiments, Pascal maintained that any appeal to some esoteric matter (instead of a true vacuum) was unsubstantiated. After explaining his various experiments, he concluded: "After having demonstrated that none of the substances perceived by our senses and known by us fills this apparently empty space, I shall think, until I am shown the existence of a substance filling it, that it is really empty and void of all matter."[4]

Pascal pointed out that a conformity of all the facts to a hypothesis serves only to make the hypothesis probable; a single contrary phenomenon can prove the hypothesis false. His thinking on the role of theory and evidence with respect to the vacuum is still greatly admired by philosophers of science as an accomplished statement of correct scientific methodology.

For Pascal, the phenomena of careful experimentation must be put into a mathematical statement in order to be useful. If a principle of nature has been discovered, it can then be verified at any time by other kinds of experiments. This is why Pascal was so thorough in his experiments and why he formulated his findings into statements about the uniform actions of air pressure and liquids. In his 1648 *Account of the Great Experiment Concerning the Equilibrium of Fluids, (Récit de la Grande expérience de l'équilibres des liqueurs)*, Pascal wrote:

> It is hard for me to believe that nature, which is not animate or sensitive, is capable of horror, since the passions presuppose a soul capable of feeling them, and I include much more to impute all these effects to the weight and pressure of the air, because I consider them only as particular cases of a universal proposition on the equilibrium of fluids.[5]

Pascal rejected an overly personalized notion of nature in favor of a more mathematical and empirically-based perspective. His experiments helped produce the syringe, the concept of a hydraulic pump, and the basic principles of hydrostatics (including Pascal's Principle regarding the pressure distribution of enclosed fluids).[6]

He wrote important treatises on the equilibrium of liquids and the weight of air. But, although he left notes and letters on his experimentation, he never finished his proposed treatise on the nature of the vacuum. However, his preface to that intended work remains a lucid account of his pivotal contribution to the developing scientific method of his day.

Pascal believed that the long-standing resistance to the notion of a vacuum rested on experimental deficiencies and the force of unjustified tradition. "For in all matters whose proof is by experiment and not by demonstration, no universal assertion can be made except by the general enumeration of all the parts and all the different cases."[7] Despite the rigor of Pascal's experiments and arguments, he remained open to empirical refutation. His exacting empirical method, coupled with his penchant for detailed mathematical explanation, helped develop a more mechanical and predictable view of nature that would challenge both Aristotelian/medieval teleology and the Cartesian rationalism concerning supposed natural laws.

Pascal deemed the discovery of objective truth to be the intention of scientific study:

> Whatever the weight of antiquity, truth should always have the advantage, even when newly discovered, since it is always older than every opinion men have held about it, and only ignorance of its nature could [cause one to] imagine it began to be at the time it began to be known.[8]

Authority, reason, and observation all had distinctive, irreducible, and (ultimately) harmonious roles in the acquiring of objective scientific knowledge. In *Pensées*, Pascal later applied this basic insight regarding various ways of knowing to his analysis of religious rationality and authority. In the case of Christianity, he argues that revelation, reason, and experience all contribute in different ways to justifying religious belief.

After his dramatic "second conversion," Pascal did not pursue mathematics or science as intensely as previously. Part of the reason for this may have been increasingly poor health along with his desire to produce his *Apology for the Christian Religion*. Moreover, he seemed to associate his former successes in math and science with his struggle with pride. Nevertheless, in 1658 during a sleepless night due to a terrible toothache, he turned his attention to a mathematical puzzle called the cycloid, which concerns the curve made by a point on the circumference of a circle traveling over a flat surface. Pascal published the piece and issued a challenge with a monetary reward to others to outdo his calculations. The fact that Pascal won the competition (only two others entered) is less important than the contribution the publication made to the development of integral calculus.

The Limits of Science

Pascal came to have a keen appreciation of the limits of science, even as he himself was expanding its powers both theoretically and practically. He believed that while we can gain from the scientific writings of the ancients, their findings are only tentative and subject to revision, as are the theories of any scientist.

Pascal, the successful scientist, marvels in the *Pensées* over the vastness of the universe. He saw it not as a cache to be unlocked but as a cosmos supercharged with mysteries high, wide, and deep—incorrigible enigmas that should startle and baffle even the most gifted scientist. Although Pascal had conducted fruitful and ground-breaking experiments, he nevertheless did not view experimentation or theorizing as ultimately unlocking the essence of nature or of God.

Many of the fragments of *Pensées* express Pascal's understanding of human limitations due to our finitude, frailties and failings. His reflections on the cosmos are intended to induce a kind of anxiety and a search for certainty beyond the limits of what science and human reason by itself can attain.

Pascal ponders at length our "disproportionality" in one long fragment of *Pensées* (199/72; subsequent quotations will be from this fragment, unless noted). Humans are strangely situated between "nothingness and infinity." Pascal's wonderment, awe and even fear are directed at the infinitely small and the infinitely great, both of which ultimately resist our finite comprehension. Regarding the macrocosm, he says, "the whole visible world is only an imperceptible dot in nature's ample bosom. No idea comes near it." He also describes "nature" as "an infinite sphere, whose centre is everywhere and circumference nowhere. In short, it is the greatest perceptible mark of God's omnipotence that our imagination should lose itself in that thought." Elsewhere he writes: "The eternal silence of these infinite spaces fills me with dread" (202/206). This sentence would likely have been put into the mouth of an unbeliever as part of a dialogue, if the *Apology* had been finished. It probably was not the response of Pascal himself. Nevertheless, it captures the feeling of human insignificance and of being overwhelmed by the immensities of nature, as does this fragment: "How many kingdoms know nothing of us!" (42/207).

Regarding the microcosm, Pascal asks us to attempt to fathom a mite whose already minute body may be divided into even more minute parts. What could be considered the "ultimate minuteness in nature"—

21

the smallest part of a tiny insect—instead reveals "a new abyss" of even smaller parts. He invites us to lose ourselves "in wonders astonishing in their minuteness as the others in their amplitude." Pascal finds "man in nature" as "a nothing compared with the infinite, a whole compared to the nothing, a middle point between all and nothing." Yet this mean is not a comfortable midpoint or an ideal situation for intellectual enterprise, but rather entails a distressing ignorance of both the microcosm and the macrocosm. "Such being as we have conceals from us the knowledge of first principles, which arise from nothingness, and the smallness of our being hides infinity from our sight." Although the microscope and telescope increased scientific knowledge in Pascal's day as never before, he nevertheless found final comfort or satisfaction in neither. Both left him mystified between the imponderables that lay both beneath and beyond our intellectual ken.

For Pascal, one of the most knowledgeable people of his day, what often passes for knowledge may be more like presumption. Humanity's unaided reasoning and perception gives out at crucial and unavoidable junctures. If someone realizes his finite vantage point, he "will tremble at [nature's] marvels. I believe that with his curiosity changing into wonder he will be more disposed to contemplate them in silence than investigate them with presumption."

Even our knowledge of the middle realm, Pascal claims, is affected by these abysmal and incorrigible infinities, no matter how much our knowledge may increase or our scientific methods may improve. Because of the interconnectedness of nature, Pascal maintains that it is equally "impossible to know the parts without knowing the whole as to know the whole without knowing the individual parts." Although we are not banished to utter skepticism, neither can we, by unaided reason and observation, ever hope to penetrate the ultimate secrets of nature. Reason must be humbled, not humiliated. Pascal states that in our natural condition we are "incapable of certain knowledge or absolute ignorance" (131/434).

Pascal did not reject reason, experimentation, or observation as vain or arrogant or futile in all cases, yet he saw human "disproportionality" as circumscribing the realm of the known in ways that would have been unacceptable to the more optimistic or messianic proponents of the scientific revolution, such as Francis Bacon (1561-1626). Bacon reckoned that science's capacities were boundless. Pascal, however, affirmed that thought—whatever its limits or pretensions—places humans over the rest of nature; so he exclaimed, somewhat hyperbolically, that "all human dignity consists in thought" (200/347). Yet, marveling at a sublime and inscrutable universe, Pascal asks:

> What else can [one] do, then, but perceive some semblance of the middle of things, eternally hopeless of knowing either their principles or their end? All things have come out of nothingness and are carried onwards to infinity. Who can follow these astonishing processes? The author of these wonders understands them; no one else can.

Pascal as a scientist could convincingly conclude that nature did not abhor a vacuum, and could account for it by discerning the principles of air pressure and the nature of liquids; he could also solve mathematical riddles ingeniously. Notwithstanding, Pascal as an observer of the universe could take little consolation in these facts, in view of the spectacle of the infinitely great and the infinitely small. Pascal as an inventor could conceive of and supervise the construction of an adding machine; Pascal as a finite being could not even add up the infinite parts of a single mite. Pascal, scientist and Christian, has no illusions about the powers of science, dependent as they are on the human constitution and its placement in nature.

Pascal believed that the kind of reasoning used in geometry and the sciences could tell us little about human nature and morality. In a fragment called "vanity of science," he wrote: "Knowledge of physical science will not console me for ignorance of morality in time of affliction, but knowledge of morality will always console me for ignorance of physical science" (22/367). Pascal's vast knowledge of mathematics and science could do little to console him in his many afflictions, but even the scientifically illiterate could find consolation in their moral bearings. The state of the soul was more relevant than astronomy: "I agree that Copernicus' opinions need not be more closely examined. But this: It affects our whole life to know whether the soul is mortal or immortal" (164/218).

Despite his achievements in science, Pascal deemed it quite limited in its ability to explain the human condition.

> I had spent a long time studying abstract sciences, and I was put off them by seeing how little one could communicate about them. When I began the study of man I saw that these abstract sciences are not proper to man, and that I was straying further from my true condition by going into them than were others by being ignorant of them (687/144).

23

This represents a change in Pascal's intellectual focus and a new perspective on scientific endeavor. It also intimates a conception that runs through the *Pensées* and elsewhere concerning the three orders of reality. The order of the body—or what science can properly study by its methods—is not the order of the mind. They are distinct, but interrelated, realms of being that require disparate methods of inquiry. In a mathematical writing, Pascal recognized these discontinuities between different kinds of figures: "points add nothing to lines, nor lines to planes, nor planes to solids."[9] Points, lines, and planes each have their own order and cannot be reduced to one another. He elaborated on this theme of discontinuity and hierarchy in describing the body, mind, and charity.

> Out of all bodies together we could not succeed in creating one little thought. It is impossible, and of a different order. Out of all bodies and minds we could not extract one impulse of true charity. It is impossible, and of a different, supernatural order (308/793).

Pascal would be the first to speak against the claims of sociobiologists, such as Edward O. Wilson, or evolutionary psychologists, such as Stephen Pinker, who insist that human behavior is exhaustively explicable in scientific terms. They claim that humans are no more than animals who can ultimately be reduced to the out-workings of mindless natural laws. Pascal thought that a materialistic and mechanistic analysis of the human person could never fully account for consciousness or for contact with a supernatural order of love or the heart. The battle between reductionists and theists continues.[10]

A Sacrifice of Intellect?

Did Pascal crucify science in the name of religion? Bertrand Russell (who echoes Nietzsche) charged that "Pascal sacrificed his magnificent mathematical intellect to his God, thereby attributing to Him a barbarity which was a cosmic enlargement of Pascal's morbid mental tortures."[11]

But Pascal did not sacrifice his mathematical intellect. After his "second conversion," Pascal shifted the focus of his intellectual endeavors to a defense of the Christian faith, and became less occupied with experimentation and mathematical projects. He was well accomplished in mathematics, and did not seem to regret or spurn his achievements. He did, however, come to see natural science from a broader perspective. Pascal's discoveries on the cycloid occurred during this time and were well publicized. His work on the omnibus was a case of applied science or technology in service of his religious ideals to benefit the poor.

The claim that Pascal attributed to God a "barbarity which was a cosmic enlargement" of his own torment reflects the projection theory of religion, which claims that God only exists as a subjective wish or desire. This sort of claim was marshaled by Nietzsche and later by Freud and Marx. Projection arguments typically beg the question of God's objective existence, and then attempt to explain why so many believe in a nonexistent being.[12] The value of Pascal's case for religious belief is explored in the rest of this book. Russell omitted it from his massive opus.

---

[1] Donald Adamson, *Blaise Pascal: Mathematician, Physicist and Thinker About God* (New York: St. Martin's Press, 1995), 3.

[2] Cited in Marvin O'Connell, *Blaise Pascal: Reasons of the Heart* (Grand Rapids, MI: Eerdmans, 1997), 26.

[3] Adamson, 14-15.

[4] Blaise Pascal, "New Experiments Concerning the Vacuum," trans. Richard Scofield in *Pascal: Great Books of the Western World* 33 (Chicago: Encyclopedia Britannica, 1952), 364.

[5] Blaise Pascal, "Account of the Great Experiment Concerning the Equilibrium of Fluids," in Ibid., 383.

[6] See Adamson, 32-33.

[7] Ibid., 358.

[8] Ibid.

[9] Quoted in Morris Bishop, *Pascal: The Life of Genius* (Westport, Connecticut: Greenwood Press Publishers, 1968), 290.

[10] See J.P. Moreland and Scott Rae, *Body and Soul* (Downers Grove, IL: InterVarsity Press, 2000).

[11] Bertrand Russell, *A History of Western Philosophy* (New York: Simon and Schuster, 1972; orig. pub. 1945), 768.

[12] See Alvin Plantinga, *Warranted Christian Belief* (New York: Oxford University Press, 2000), 135-163.

4

Theological Controversy

> The Jesuits have tried to combine God and the world, and have only earned the contempt of God and the world. For, as regards conscience, this is evident, and as regards the world, they are no good at intrigue (988/488).

This barb from *Pensées* is an apt example of Pascal's antipathy for the Jesuits. Writing on behalf of the Jansenists of Port-Royal, who were under heavy fire from the Jesuits, he secretly composed and published eighteen *Provincial Letters* (*Lettres Provinciales)* concerning the ethics and theology of the powerful Jesuit institution, which had formed in the wake of the Reformation to defend the pope and Catholicism. The letters became classics of French literature.

Seventeenth century France was a world where religious controversy had severe implications. There was no First Amendment to grant religious liberty and reduce church-state feuds. Religious matters were not strictly private. Relativism, and its resulting indifference to religious claims, was not the force then that it is today. The French government could enforce religious behavior. The perspective at this time was generally that "king and faith and lawful government stood or fell together."[1] Not long after Pascal's death, the French government would raze Port-Royal des Champes because it lost a key theological controversy—a controversy in which Pascal was passionately involved.

Jesuits and Jansenists

Jansenism is often portrayed as almost Protestant because of its emphasis on human depravity, the need for God's grace in salvation, the rigors of the authentic Christian life, and divine predestination.

26

Nevertheless, its founders and propagators (Pascal included) were not crypto-Protestants, however much they debated with the defenders of Rome, the Jesuits. The Jansenists wanted reform from within, not schism—although their enemies sometimes insulted them by calling them "Calvinists." The movement's originator was Cornelius Jansen (1585-1638), a Dutch theologian who wrote a massive tome, *Augustinius*, published in 1639 after his death. Jansen's ideas were furthered by Saint-Cyran (1581-1643).

The ideas and practices of Jansenism had taken root at Port-Royal, where Jacqueline Pascal was now a nun and where Blaise sometimes stayed after his second conversion. Antoine Arnauld (1612-1694), known as "the Great Arnauld" because of his writings on theology, logic, and other topics, was a kind of theologian-in-residence at the abbey. His 1643 book *On Frequent Communion* (*De la fréquent communion*) set out Jansenist teachings in a popular way and was influential. But he was in trouble with the influential Jesuits, whom he opposed for their moral laxness and their human-centered religion.

Arnauld and others at Port-Royal des Champes enlisted Pascal to assist them in their theological and moral battles. They knew that he possessed a keen mind and that he could communicate winsomely with people outside of the theological elite. Pascal was given a crash course on moral theology. The tutors may also have contributed to the substance of his letters against the Jesuits. In January 1656, under the name of Louis de Montalte, Pascal began to write letters to a friend "in the provincials" concerning the recent attacks on the Jansenists, Jesuit moral thinking, and their respective concepts of grace and salvation.[2] Pascal used satire in a fictional exchange of letters in a strikingly original manner.[3]

The first three letters were a last-gasp attempt to save Arnauld from being condemned as heretical by the Sorbonne theological faculty at the University of Paris. Arnauld would be deprived of his doctorate and expelled from this august body. Nevertheless, Pascal began to draw the public into a debate that previously had been only a matter of rarified academic interest. He would go on to write fifteen additional letters, ending in March 1657. The eighteen letters became very popular, given their originality, humor, satire, intelligence, and panache. A fragment from a nineteenth letter exists, but was not published at the time of the disputes.

The substance of these letters addressed two interrelated items of morality and doctrine. The first focused on the practice of confession and absolution. Roman Catholic doctrine, unlike Protestant theology, required communicants to confess their sins to special priests, called confessors. The Jansenists accused the Jesuits of diluting the idea of sin in order to fit worldly tastes. This rendered repentance and true faith unnecessary. Since the crown had become more religious since the death of Cardinal Richelieu (1642), some of the French wanted to adopt a dab of religion in order to impress the government, but without too much genuine devotion .

The Catholic Church divided sins into specific categories with attendant penance requirements. Absolution required an assessment of the nature of sins committed and the assignment of the penance appropriate to them. The assessment of the severity of past sins was part of the religious casuistry, which concerned the application of broad moral rules to particular situations. Casuistry also addresses the discernment of specific obligations to general rules, which is the focus of a spiritual *director*. A *confessor* emphasizes the interpretation of past actions and prescribes penance, as opposed to giving specific moral advice for the future. However, if one knew that a chosen confessor was especially lenient, this could encourage looser living. Conversely, if one's confessor was known to be more strict, this would favor a more circumspect way of life.

Some Jesuit confessors advanced a view of assessing sin called probablism. If a few Jesuit doctors, or even one, ruled in one's favor on a moral matter (say, telling a lie in a situation), one could appropriate this judgment for one's own situation, even if the weight of traditional opinion was against it. This school of casuistry was the most lenient option available. Probablism allowed for any interpretation, however *improbable*, as long as one doctor of the church—and this usually meant a Jesuit—had advanced it.[4] Alternatively, "tutiorism," advocated by the Jansenists, required strict adherence to the letter of the law as the safest and most holy course to follow. Unlike probablism, it assessed morality in terms of what the overwhelming majority of church authorities had pronounced on an issue. A tutiorist confessor had a far sharper eye for sin and more demanding standards for penance.

In his fifth letter, Pascal presents a fictional dialogue to explain the doctrine of probablism, which addresses whether one can waive one's responsibility to fast during Lent if skipping dinner makes it difficult to sleep. The confessor tells his subject that he can omit fasting during Lent because a book published in 1626 called *Moral Theology on the Basis of Twenty-four Casuists* by the Spanish Jesuit Antonio Escobar allows for it—and for just about any other remotely extenuating circumstance. The confessor quotes one Fr. Bauny to the effect that "One must not refuse absolution to those who remain in proximate occasions of sin, if they are so placed that they cannot turn from their ways without giving rise to gossip or bringing on themselves some inconvenience thereby."[5]

The confessor goes on to cite a source that even allows one to seek out occasions to sin "when the spiritual or temporal good of ourselves or our neighbour leads us to do so." The earnest penitent then objects, "What, Father! Because they put these three lines into their books, it has become permissible to seek occasions of sin? I thought that the only rule to be followed was Scripture and the tradition of the church, but not your casuists." To this, the confessor replies, "Good Lord!. . . . You remind me of those Jansenists." The subject exclaims, "I am not satisfied with probability. I want certainty." The confessor then explains "the doctrine of probable opinions," which is "the foundation and ABC of all our moral teaching."[6] Quoting again from an authoritative book, he says, "An opinion is probable when it is founded on reasons of some importance. Whence it sometimes happens that one really grave doctor can make an opinion probable."[7] The upshot of this dialogue is stated by the penitent: "In other words, Father, your arrival has meant the disappearance of St Augustine, St Chrysostom, St Ambrose, St Jerome and the others as far as morality is concerned," and these have been replaced by "modern authors" of dubious moral sobriety.[8]

Earlier in the same letter, Pascal excoriates the Jesuits for their doctrine of "mental reservation," whereby one is excused from an evil action if one claims to mean something else by it. This doctrine, developed by Escobar, stipulates that the moral value of an action is found not in the deed itself but in the mental attitude of the agent performing the deed. One might be allowed to lie by attributing another meaning to one's words than what would be understood by the person listening to them. This might remind Americans of the events surrounding the impeachment of President Bill Clinton in 1999. Consider his creative use of the words "sex" and "is." His "mental intention" differed from what was commonly understood to be the meaning of these terms.

Using an ingenious interview format, Pascal allows the Jesuit interlocutor to be hoisted by his own theological petard. By letter ten, the hapless confessor has justified nearly every sin—including simony, usury, drunkenness, theft, slander, and even murder in some cases—and he has, of course, justified every sinner. Contrition is not required for absolution; only premeditated, deliberate sins (and not always those) are held against the sinner; and no moral exertion is laid upon the penitent (apart from consenting to the clever machinations of the confessor). What, then, is left of religion? After another convoluted explanation of casuistry, the confessor utters the unforgivable claim Pascal has been intimating in every letter: "This is how our [Jesuit] Fathers have dispensed men from their irksome obligation of actually loving God. And this doctrine has so many advantages that our Fathers...have vigorously defended it against attempts to attack it."[9]

Pascal's seeker lets his indignation fly. The statement is filled with biblical citations and denunciations. Here is a taste of it.

> You break the "great commandment on which hang all the law and the prophets" [Matthew 22:40], you attack piety in its heart; you take away the spirit that gives it life; you say that the love of God is not necessary to salvation; and you even go so far as to claim that "this dispensation from loving God is the advantage that Christ brought to the world." This is the height of impiety. The price of Christ's blood shall be to win for us the dispensation from loving him; but "since God so loves the world that he gave his only begotten Son" [John 3:16], the world redeemed by him shall be exempted from loving him! Strange theology for our times.[10]

The debate as to whether Pascal was fair to the Jesuits' casuistry has raged ever since the publication of *The Provincial Letters*, and cannot be settled here. Nonetheless, it should be noted that Pascal was always a thorough interpreter of documents. Because the stakes were high, it is unlikely that he terribly misrepresented his opponents. He remarks:

> People ask if I have myself read all the books I quote.—I reply that I have not; it would certainly have meant spending my life reading very bad books; but I read Escobar right through twice; and, as for the others, I got my friends to read them, but I did not use a single passage without reading it myself in the book quoted, going into the context involved, and reading the passage before and after it, to avoid all risk of quoting an objection as an answer, which would have been reprehensible and unjust.[11]

Although Pascal's attempt to vindicate Jansenism failed politically, some abuses of Jesuit casuistry were later admitted by the church.[12] The term "casuistry" today tends to mean the practice of irrelevant or self-justifying distinctions; it is sometimes deemed synonymous with "sophistry." The adjective "jesuitical" is not infrequently taken to mean selfishly crafty or cunning with respect to small details.

The Relevance of Casuistry

This seventeenth-century feud brings to the fore the enduring question of the relationship of broad moral principles to specific rules and situations. This is the nature of casuistry (without any pejorative connotations), which an assortment of philosophers and theologians have tackled through the ages.

Casuistry is also important to philosophers who are not primarily concerned with religious themes. For example, G.E. Moore, the British analytic philosopher, underscored the pertinence of casuistry in his influential work *Principia Ethica* (1903).

> Casuistry may indeed be *more* particular and ethics *more* general; but that means that they differ in degree and not in kind. . . . Casuistry, not content with the general law that charity is a virtue, must attempt to discover the relative merits of every different form of charity. Casuistry forms, therefore, part of the ideal of ethical science: Ethics cannot be complete without it.[13]

For example, if loving others is deemed supremely valuable in ethics, then one must determine which acts are loving and which are not. Particular cases must be brought into agreement with the rule. Does the norm of loving one's neighbor rule out any military involvement, capital punishment, or abortion? These issues are questions of casuistry, as Moore understood that term.

All religions and much of ethics address casuistry. Consider the question: "Are lies ever justified?" Augustine and Kant forbade all lying as wrong (for different reasons)—even when lying would be the only way to save innocent lives. On the other hand, while the Bible declares that "You shall not give false testimony against your neighbor" (Exodus 20:16), it commends the actions of Rahab, who lied to protect God's spies from certain death (Joshua 2). Some, therefore, suggest that not all lying is bearing false witness.

Jesus blamed some of the religious authorities of his day for missing the meaning of God's law—concerning the Sabbath and financial obligations, for instance—and substituting merely human and self-excusing rules in its place. They were "the blind leading the blind," with respect to assessing past sins and giving guidance for future behavior (see Matthew 15:1-14). They were not unlike Pascal's portrait of the Jesuits.

Pascal's debate might spark some reflection on the bearing of ancient religious authority on present affairs. Modern Westerners often consider religion as something of a consumer item or even a hobby. If so, religion exists for me, and not vice versa. I am free to adapt, expand, and edit any or all religious traditions (or combine several of them, however logically incompatible they may be) to fit my "spirituality." This, in essence, is what Pascal and his theological cohorts accused the Jesuits of doing.

God's Grace and Human Effort

Pascal attacked the theology of the Jesuits as well as their ethics, particularly that of their prominent Spanish theologian, Luis de Molina (1535-1600). The item of contention was the doctrine of God's grace in relation to human salvation. The Jansenists accused the Jesuits of catering to human frailties in light of their compromised views of human sinfulness and God's providence.

Philosophers have labored over the issue of human freedom and moral responsibility with respect to causal factors beyond one's immediate control. Hence, the "free will and determinism" problem appears. Are humans controlled by forces larger than and outside of themselves, or do they have the ability—at least in noncoerced circumstances—to choose freely? What does "freedom" mean? Does it entail that one must have the power of contrary choice or does it mean that one merely needs to choose on the basis of internal reasons, even if one could not have chosen differently?

In theology, the question focuses on the causal relationship between the Creator and humans. How do the human will and the divine will interact with respect to one's salvation? For Christians, salvation means the forgiveness of sins, escape from divine judgment, and the gift of eternal life—all credited to the actions of God's grace. But how does grace produce its effects in relation to erring mortals?

The controversy in Pascal's day centered on the concepts of "sufficient grace" and "efficacious grace." The Jesuits of the Molinist school had a less pessimistic account of human nature than the Jansenists. The Molinists argued that God had provided grace sufficient to enable everyone to engage in religious practices that would merit efficacious (or saving) grace. God did not need to act specially to draw someone into salvation. As Pascal put it: "The Jesuits claim that there is a grace given generally to all, so subject to free will that this makes it efficacious or not as it chooses without any fresh assistance from God, and without anything more being needed for it to act effectively."[14] In other words, normal human effort was enough to secure salvation.

The Jansenists thought this conception denied the sinfulness of humanity and also contributed to the cheapening of the Christian life, since spiritual seriousness was not required for being a Christian. The Jansenists claimed that all people are congenitally and chronically prone to hell-meriting sin, which can only be overcome by efficacious grace, which cannot be resisted. As Pascal explained: "But to free the soul from worldly affections, to remove it from what it holds dear, to make it die unto itself, to bring and unite it solely and immutably to God, this can only be the work of an almighty hand."[15] However, the Jansenists differed from the Calvinists by claiming that efficacious grace was not irrevocable. God might withdraw it.

Pascal addressed the questions of God's providence, human freedom, grace, and salvation especially in his eighteenth letter. He distanced himself from both the Calvinists and the Molinists and sided with what he took to be Augustine's view of Scripture.

> The only way of reconciling these apparent contradictions which ascribe our good deed now to God and now to ourselves is to recognize that, as St Augustine says, 'our deeds are our own, because of the free will producing them, and they are also God's, because of his grace, causing our free will to produce them.' And as he says elsewhere, God makes us do what he pleases by making us desire what we might not desire.[16]

This controversy highlights the perennial philosophical and theological subject of human freedom and responsibility. Pascal argued for what is now called "compatiblism." One need not have the power of contrary choice in order to choose authentically between options. One may choose "freely" so long as one is not coerced or put under undue duress, as when a gun is pointed at the head. Therefore, external determination and personal freedom are logically compatible. Both the irreligious philosopher David Hume and the Protestant philosopher Jonathan Edwards, for example, held to this view (for very different reasons). Conversely, the Jesuits claimed that power of contrary choice is required for human freedom and moral responsibility, and that it had not been lost through the fall of humans into sin (contra Augustine and

Pascal). This view today is called "libertarianism" (not to be confused with the political philosophy, Libertarianism) or incompatiblism (external determination and personal freedom are incompatible). This sentiment was held by the Protestant theologian Jacob Arminius (against John Calvin) and is advanced by many philosophers and theologians today. The question of free will and divine providence appears significantly in *Pensées* also.

Pascal's defense of a theologically-oriented compatiblism against the libertarianism of the Jesuits helps elucidate several important themes for philosophers in the areas of metaphysics (the powers of the human will in relation to God), ethics (the ethical demands placed upon us and how we are able to respond to them), and epistemology (knowing the nature and limits of human will and goodness in relation to God).

The End of the Battle

Despite the popular appeal of *The Provincial Letters* in France and elsewhere, the powers-that-be were not convinced of the Jansenist cause. Even a church-accredited miracle could not stop the juggernaut set against it. In April of 1656, Pascal's young niece was reportedly healed at Port-Royal of an untreatable and festering fistula of the eye after being touched by a holy relic. Pascal and others took this to be a supernatural sign of God's favor upon the Jansenist cause.

Miracle or not, *The Provincial Letters* were placed on the Index of Forbidden Books in 1657. The Jansenist abbey would soon fall. Because of the distress over Jansenism, Blaise's younger sister, Jacqueline, died in 1661 at the age of thirty-six. The surviving nuns, much to their distress, were later required to sign official statements disavowing their allegiance to Jansenism. On the order of Louis XIV, Port-Royal was razed in 1710 and its inhabitants—who had been given fifteen minutes to leave—were scattered among various convents. Its cemetery was plowed over and the graves of its nuns were disinterred and the remains unceremoniously thrown into a common grave. Jansenism survived, however, in various forms outside of France and later within it, but it had lost the battle to be recognized as a bona fide element in the Catholic Church.

The confessors denounced by Pascal are long-forgotten. Molina is not remembered for his views on grace and salvation, but for his metaphysical doctrine of "middle knowledge," a sophisticated understanding of divine omniscience and human choice, which has been recently embraced by many analytic philosophers of religion.[17] *The Provincial Letters*, on the other hand, are still known and loved everywhere.

---

[1] Marvin O'Connell, *Blaise Pascal: Reasons of the Heart* (Grand Rapids, MI: Eerdmans, 1997), 122.

[2] Although Pascal defended the Jansenist cause in *The Provincial Letters* and resided at Port-Royal des Champes for a time, he was never an official member. He seemed to diverge from Jansenist doctrine at a few points in *Pensées* (see 911/781; 912/781).

[3] See Donald Adamson, *Blaise Pascal: Mathematician, Physicist and Thinker About God* (New York: St. Martins Press, 1995), 89.

[4] Ibid., 142.

[5] Pascal, Blaise, *The Provincial Letters*, trans. A. J. Krailsheimer. New York: Penguin Books, 1967, 81.

[6] Ibid.

[7] Ibid., 82.

[8] Ibid., 86.

[9] Ibid., 160.

[10] Ibid., 161-162. I have added to the text the biblical references.

[11] Blaise Pascal, *Pensées*, ed. Alban Krailsheimer (New York: Penguin, 1966), "Sayings Attributed to Pascal," 355-356. See Adamson, 85-114 for a defense of the truthfulness of Pascal's case.

[12] See Adamson, 113-114.

[13] G.E. Moore, *Principia Ethica* (London: Cambridge University Press, 1978), 4-5.

[14] Pascal, *Provincial Letters*, 41.

[15] Ibid., 78.

[16] Ibid., 284.

[17] For a contemporary defense of this view, see William Lane Craig, *God Only Wise* (Eugene, OR: Wipf and Stock Publishers, 2000).

5

The Character and
Plan of the *Pensées*

The last act is bloody, however fine the rest of the play. They
throw earth over your head and it is finished for ever (165/210).

We plunder the effects of the great, seeking ways to prolong
their presence in the world of the living. We refuse to let them go. The
influence of the great writers is not "finished forever." Yet those
departed cannot oversee the rummaging of their works. Their
intentions—if known—are often neglected or even contradicted. The
scavenging results are generally mixed; we find gems and some less
than luminous effects.

Framing the Fragments of Genius

The relatives of Blaise Pascal faced a formidable literary task
after his death in 1662. Although he was chronically sick and
debilitated in his last years, the doctors did not imagine his final illness
was the "sickness unto death." Pascal's relatives and friends did know
of his proposed defense of Christianity, to be called *An Apology for the
Christian Religion*, which he never finished. Whether Pascal had
abandoned the project or whether he simply ran out of time and energy
is difficult to determine, although I favor the latter theory. In any case,
Pascal left a mass of unfinished materials intended for the *Apology*.
This project probably began to gel in 1658, when Pascal gave a
lecture on his proposed defense to scholars at Port-Royal (see 149/430).
Several years before his death he began jotting notes regarding the

36

work. He only resorted to writing his thoughts after his prodigious memory began failing. Previously, he would formulate ideas completely, then write them out in a torrent of energy.

In the preface to the first edition of *Pensées*, published in 1669, Etienne Periér, Pascal's brother-in-law and compatriot in scientific investigation, complained that Pascal's notes were uneven in quality, unorganized, and difficult to decipher. Nevertheless, the collection was published in the best form the executors could muster. A copy of a table of contents written by Pascal, was confirmed to be authentic in 1953; it demonstrated that Pascal had arranged some of his notes into twenty-eight chapters containing a total of 382 entries.[1] However, he left some 590 other entries unclassified. This discovery did not solve every textual or organizational problem, but it does put a significant number of fragments into the order Pascal intended.

A variety of numbering systems and classifications have been used for the *Pensées*. The two most prominent numbering systems are those of Brunschvicg (used in the Harvard Classics and Great Books editions) and Lafuma (used in the Penguin classic edition). The latter recreates Pascal's original intention concerning the first 382 fragments, originally arranged in bundles of notes. Houston[2] and Levi[3] have come up with new arrangements. Some fragments not meant for the finished apology have been published in the Penguin edition.

Early editions of *Pensées* did not include skeptical or seemingly nihilistic fragments, probably because the editors knew that these fragments did not represent Pascal's mature thinking and because they could not decipher what purpose these fragments would have served in the *Apology*. His survivors surmised that these puzzling thoughts might mislead the reader to think that Pascal held views unworthy of him. When all the fragments were incorporated into later versions of *Pensées*, their fears were realized. (One reason Pascal is sometimes seen as existentialist is that fragments expressing the ideas of alienated unbelievers are taken as his own thoughts.)

Pascal would likely have placed some of the more haunting passages into the mouth of a skeptical interlocutor as part of a dialogue constructed to move the unbeliever from anxious doubt to certain faith.

> When I consider the brief span of my life absorbed into the eternity which comes before and after [and] the small space I occupy and which I see swallowed up in the infinite immensity of spaces of which I know nothing and which know nothing of me, I take fright and am amazed to see myself here rather than

there: there is no reason for me to be here rather than there, now rather than then. Who put me here? (68/205).

This dizzying reflection on human contingency is not the voice of Pascal the apologist, but of Pascal's interlocutor. Pascal's proposed *Apology* would have involved several dialogues and letters. The odds are it would not have been a long, didactic treatise. This is evident from some of the fragments themselves where Pascal notes that he should compose a "*letter to induce men to seek God.* Then make them look for him among the philosophers, sceptics, and dogmatists, who will worry the man who seeks" (4/184). Some fragments of propose dialogues:

> 'Why, do you not say yourself that the sky and the birds prove God?'—'No.'—'Does your religion not say so?'—'No. For though it is true in a sense for some souls whom God has enlightened in this way, yet it is untrue for the majority' (3/244).

The last sections of the famous wager argument are in a dialogue format as well (418/233).

To discern the meaning and placement of the fragments, one must pick up on some clues left by Pascal.

> First part: Wretchedness of man without God. Second part: Happiness of man with God. [Or:] First part: Nature is corrupt, proved by nature itself. Second part: There is a Redeemer, proved by Scripture (6/60).

Pascal completed much more of the first part than the second, which was left in a rather unorganized and fragmentary state. Despite this limitation, Pascal bequeathed us with a wealth of material, particularly on the vagaries and vicissitudes of the human condition. Pascal's organized files were bundled into four basic sections. He first argues that human reason left to itself cannot understand the greatness and misery of the human condition. Second, the philosophers have not be able to deliver sustained happiness to the bemused human race. Third, only Christianity accounts for the human condition as both great and miserable. Material in the fourth bundle addresses the historical arguments for the divine authority of the Bible.

Unlike the *Provincial Letters*, *Pensées* does engage in a polemic against religious disputants, but in apologetics directed at the sort of unbelievers Pascal knew during his worldly period: the well-endowed sophisticates more concerned with their careers and status in polite society than in developing any ardor for religion. Pascal's apology was not meant as a general manual for the defense of Christian faith, as was Thomas Aquinas's *Summa Contra Gentiles* four hundred years earlier. Nevertheless, *Pensées* has garnered a perennial appeal.

Pascal's Distinctive Method

Christian apologetics in Pascal's day was heavily influenced by a Cartesian approach, which reasoned in a geometrical fashion from clear and distinct first principles to Christian conclusions. Pascal knew geometry better than most, and never belittled its power. Nevertheless, he deemed it inadequate for drawing an unbeliever toward faith. Pascal had in mind a new manner of defending an ancient faith. He wrote, "Let no one say that I have said nothing new; the arrangement of the material is new. In playing tennis both players use the same ball, but one plays it better" (696/22).

Pascal appeals to what he calls "the intuitive mind," which apprehends numerous, intricate principles leading to a particular perspective (512/1). However, he does not abandon the virtues of the mathematical mind, since he does define terms and argue according to logical principles. Although his presentation is not deductive or straightforwardly linear, he employs a variety of converging arguments, all with the same end in view.[4]

Pascal labored to introduce, step by step, a new perspective for his unbelieving reader, one which would illuminate previously shadowy or opaque terrain by explaining the ultimate issues of life and death more comprehensively and compellingly than the other worldviews. This would make the Christian outlook appealing to one seeking answers to the mysteries of existence. He also aimed to jolt the complacent out of their indolence by emphasizing the need to pursue earnestly religious matters because of the high stakes involved.

Pascal skillfully wields a trademark philosophical strategy throughout the *Pensées* on a number of topics. It is a peculiar kind of dialectic. He presents two mutually exclusive claims on a subject, both of which command some respect and both of which seem true from one perspective. But without a larger perspective, which conserves their genuine insights but does not endorse their limitations, the two claims cancel each other out and leave the issue and the inquirer in darkness.

Knowing God without knowing our own wretchedness makes for pride. Knowing our own wretchedness without knowing God makes for despair. Knowing Jesus Christ strikes the balance because he shows us both God and our own wretchedness (192/527).

The first two ideas concerning God and our wretchedness are partial truths: there is a God and we are wretched. But without a larger framework one falls into either the error of presumption (God *sans* wretchedness) or the error of despair (wretchedness *sans* God). Knowing Jesus Christ allows us to conserve these partial truths while avoiding both pride and presumption, each of which result from absolutizing incomplete perspectives.

Similarly, Pascal opposed those who thought that human reason alone was sufficient for religious knowledge, and he also opposed those who did not bring reason to bear on religious claims. "If we submit everything to reason our religion will be left with nothing mysterious or supernatural. If we offend the principles of reason, our religion will be absurd and ridiculous" (173/273). Here are two equal and opposite errors, which require a resolution—a *tertium quid*—provided by placing them into a broader perspective. One must admit that faith receives truths through divine revelation; yet those truths are not unreasonable. "Faith certainly tells us what the senses do not, but not the contrary of what they see; it is above, not against them" (185/265). Pascal is neither against reason, nor does he deem reason sufficient for coming to know religious truth. There is a third way. Pascal does not synthesize contradictory elements. He rather reconciles them according to a higher viewpoint. He explains his method further:

> When we want to correct someone usefully and show him he is wrong, we must see from what point of view he is approaching the matter, for it is usually right from that point of view, and we must admit this, but show him the point of view from which it is wrong. This will please him, because he will see that he is not wrong but merely failed to see every aspect of the question (701/9).

But Pascal was not a relativist or radical perspectivist, such as Nietzsche, who thought that there were no facts but only interpretations. Unlike many interested in "spirituality" today, Pascal did not claim that religious truth was merely subjective or cultural. He believed that Christianity was objectively true, reasonable, and existentially compelling. Pascal's rejection of a geometric method of argumentation did not entail denying truth as something to be sought, discovered, and valued. "Truth is so obscured nowadays, and lies so well established that unless we love the truth we shall never recognize it" (739/864). Moreover, truth must have its way with us. "Weaklings are those who know the truth, but maintain it only as far as it is in their interest to do so, and apart from that forsake it" (740/583).

Pascal also knew that Christianity makes claims on the entire personality; accepting it as true is not a matter of mere intellectual assent, but of embarking on a new venture in life. Persuasion—involving and beckoning the whole person—in this case can be slippery. In a fragment labeled "inconstancy," he wrote,

> We think playing upon man is like playing upon an ordinary organ. It is indeed an organ, but strange, shifting and changeable. Those who only know how to play an ordinary organ would never be in tune on this one. You have to know where the keys are (55/111).

Pascal's goal was to strike the right chords in the right sequence to summon a soul to rectitude before reality:

> I should, therefore like to arouse in man the desire to find truth, to be ready, free from passion, to follow it wherever he may find it, realizing how far his knowledge is clouded by passions. I should like him to hate his concupiscence which automatically makes his decisions for him, so that it should not blind him when he makes his choice, nor hinder him once he has chosen (119/423).

This project often appealed to the three orders of existence, which Pascal applied in a number of ways.

Pascal's Three Orders

In developing his three orders of being and knowing, Pascal expanded on a mathematical insight concerning the discontinuity between the realms of lines, squares, and cubes, and applied it to the body, the mind, and the heart. Pascal believed in the metaphysical distinction of body and mind, but he went beyond Descartes in speaking of the heart as well. Each of these orders "has its own faculty of apprehension, its own objects of importance, and its own principles of judgment."[5]

The order of the body concerns the senses' apprehension of objects and phenomena (whether nature abhors a vacuum); it trades on empirical principles and observations. Those dominated by the order of the body have no interest in things intellectual or spiritual: "The greatness of intellectual people is not visible to kings, rich men, captains, who are all great in a carnal sense" (308/793). But the sphere of the body should be kept in perspective: "All bodies, the firmament, the stars, the earth and its kingdoms are not worth the least of minds, for it knows them all and itself too, while bodies know nothing (308/793).

The mind's province concerns rational principles and calculations. Those defined by the order of the mind do not need physical or social greatness. "Great geniuses have their power, their splendour, their greatness, their victory, and their lustre, and do not need carnal greatness" (308/793). However, those gifted in the use of reason may miss out on the realities of faith, which, while not opposed to reason, emanate from a realm beyond the ken of unaided human rationality. Pascal claims that reason rightly employed divines its own limitations rationally: "Reason's last step is the recognition that there are an infinite number of things which are beyond it. It is merely feeble if it does not go so far as to recognize that" (188/267). In his reflections on the infinitely large and small, Pascal highlights the limitations of the finite knower in relation to the universe (199/72). "If natural things are beyond it, what are we to say about supernatural things?" (188/267)

When Pascal speaks of the meaning and role of "reason," he usually uses the term to refer specifically to discursive argumentation—that is, the method by which one establishes the truth of a conclusion from the truth of premises. Pascal's frequent comments on the limits or "humbling" of "reason" concerning our knowledge of God and the supernatural have this particular concept of "reason" in mind, which differs from the broader Scholastic-Aristotelian concept of reason.[6]

The order of the heart (or charity) addresses items of knowledge and wisdom not knowable through observation or rational calculation, such as unprovable but certain first principles concerning numbers, space, and time; it is also the channel for emotional, aesthetic, and religious experience (110/282). Matters of love, for example, are neither items of scientific observation nor rational calculation. The heart is the faculty whereby we can know of supernatural things pertaining to God and salvation. Neither science nor unaided reason can lead us to this realm. Although Pascal marvels at Jesus' ability to teach profound truths simply and clearly (309/797), and never depreciates his intellect, he sees him as supernaturally revealing the order of the heart.

> Jesus without wealth or any outward show of knowledge has his own order of holiness. He made no discoveries; he did not reign, but he was humble, patient, thrice holy to God, terrible to devils, and without sin. With what great pomp and marvelously magnificent array he came in the eyes of the heart, which perceive wisdom (308/793).

Yet reason still has a vital role to play in defending faith. It is necessary in helping to convince the reluctant unbeliever of Christianity; but it is insufficient in itself to bring anyone to faith, which is a gift of God and a matter of the heart. Nevertheless, apologetic argumentation may serve to remove important obstacles to faith in order to make the unbeliever more receptive to a source of vital knowledge beyond the reach of human reasoning when left to itself. [7]

Before we test Pascal's case for faith, we need to scrutinize his rejection of a staple of medieval philosophy and of Descartes' rationalism as well: natural theology—the attempt to prove the existence of God apart from divine revelation.

---

[1] Alban Krailsheimer, *Pascal* (New York: Hill and Wang, 1980), 41, and Alban Krailsheimer, "Introduction," Blaise Pascal, *Pensées*, ed. Krailsheimer (New York: Penguin, 1966), 19.

[2] Blaise Pascal, *The Mind on Fire: An Anthology of the Writings of Blaise Pascal*, ed. James Houston (Minneapolis, MN: Bethany Press, 1997). Houston arranges the *Pensées* fragments as a Christian apologetic.

[3] Blaise Pascal, *Pensées and Other Writings*, trans. Honor Levi, intro and notes by Anthony Levi (New York: Oxford University Press, 1995). Levi's annotations raise significant issues philosophically.

[4] See Krailsheimer, "Introduction," 26.

[5] Diogenes Allen, *Three Outsiders: Kierkegaard, Pascal, Weil* (Cambridge, MA: Cowley Publications, 1983), 35.

[6] See Peter Kreeft, *Christianity for Modern Pagans: Pascal's Pensées, Edited, Outlined, and Explained* (St. Louis: Ignatius Press, 1993), 230.

[7] See Krailsheimer, "Introduction," 23.

6

God:
To Prove or Not to Prove?

It is a remarkable fact that no canonical writer has ever used nature to prove God. They all try to make people believe in him. David, Solomon, etc. never said: "there is no such thing as a vacuum, therefore God exists." They must have been cleverer than the cleverest of their successors, all of whom have used proofs from nature. This is very noteworthy (463/243).

The plan of the *Apology for the Christian Religion* was distinctive in that it did not include the classical discipline of natural theology—the intellectual task of arguing for the existence of a monotheistic God from the evidence of nature and/or human experience. Pascal was bucking a centuries-old trend in Christian philosophy. Descartes made arguments for God's existence a central piece of his rationalistic system. Pascal thought he could defend the Christian faith without this tool. He rejected natural theology for several fascinating reasons, all of which merit some attention. This is especially so given the recent renaissance of natural theology in contemporary philosophy after a long period of near banishment. Before looking at Pascal's critique of natural theology, we should briefly explain its meaning and significance philosophically.

What is Natural Theology?

Natural theology differs from revealed theology in the theistic religions. Revealed theology concerns what can be ascertained from

44

sacred Scriptures, whether it is the Torah, the Bible, or the Koran. Natural theology does not appeal to Scripture for information about God, but rather constructs arguments for the existence of God from the data of the cosmos and the self. This endeavor, if successful, wins over the unbeliever to theistic belief of a general kind without direct appeal to Scripture. It appeals to matters already accepted by the unbeliever— such as the existence and design of the cosmos, moral intuitions, etc.— and argues from these realities to God's existence.

Natural theology has historically used several kinds of argumentative strategies. Cosmological arguments argue from cosmos to Creator. Design arguments argue from design in the universe to a Designer. Moral arguments argue from morality to a moral Law-Giver. Ontological arguments argue from the idea of God to the existence of God. Religious experience arguments argue from certain experiences to God as their cause. Suffice to say these arguments come in many shapes, strengths, and sizes.[1] By natural theology, Pascal seemed to have in mind two sorts of arguments, which he referred to as "metaphysical proofs"—arguments that appeal to facts of the universe as evidence for a being who accounts for its existence (cosmological arguments) and who designed it (design arguments). Pascal's own strategy, assessed in the following chapters, did not employ these arguments; instead he traded heavily on the human condition as evidence of the need for a Redeemer. His argument was a direct or one-step appeal to Christian theism, whereas natural theology attempts first to establish rationally the existence of a generic monotheism, after which arguments may be offered on the basis of Scripture, history, miracles, and so on. Pascal did suggest an argument for Christianity from religious experience, but even this appeals directly to Christian experience, not merely to a general theism. Why, then, did Pascal reject the traditional method—especially design and cosmological arguments—without rejecting apologetics entirely?

Rejecting Natural Theology

As the opening quotation reveals, Pascal was impressed by the absence of natural theology in Scripture. The Bible does claim that nature speaks of its Creator (Romans 1-2; Psalm 19:1-4), but one is hard pressed to find a philosophical argument for God's existence per se.[2] Since Pascal labored to be faithful to Scripture, he took this philosophical omission as normative and exemplary. If Pascal was right, the considerable work done by philosophers recently to defend cosmological, design, and other theistic arguments would seem to be theologically illegitimate, whatever their philosophical value may be.

But Pascal's observation only shows that no biblical writer deemed such arguments pertinent to their situations. This is not surprising, since atheism was not a significant issue for the biblical writers. Unbelievers were much more likely to be polytheists, pantheists, or to have another monotheistic or henotheistic god. The omission of natural theology may also indicate that from a biblical perspective, one may be justified in believing in God apart from any formal philosophical arguments for God's existence. Pascal's case against natural theology seems to be an argument from silence. Since one has difficulty finding any explicit prohibition of theistic arguments in the Bible, the absence of theistic arguments does not seem to entail that they would be forbidden or pointless for all believers in all circumstances. In a time when atheism has become a challenge to theistic faith (as in most of the world today), such arguments may prove helpful in defending the rationality of belief.[3]

But Pascal's reasons go deeper than merely noting an omission. He also maintains that the God of natural theology is too theologically and existentially thin, and much too abstract. The God derived from natural theology is not the God of the Scriptures, who created and guided the Jewish people supernaturally, who was incarnated in Jesus Christ, and who calls people to give their ultimate allegiance to him for their eternal salvation. The God of natural theology is merely the God of deism, a Creator and nothing more. Pascal's memorable line from the Memorial reads, "The God of Abraham, Isaac, and Jacob, not the God of philosophers and scholars." As he quips:

> Even if someone were convinced that the proportions between numbers are immaterial, eternal truths, depending on a first truth in which they subsist, called God, I should not consider that he had made much progress toward his salvation (449/556).

Augustinian that he was, Pascal, nevertheless, seems to be referring to—and trivializing—Augustine's argument from the existence of truth to the existence of God. Even if the argument is rationally successful, Pascal fears that it has little or no effect on the soul. It is thus apologetically and existentially mute.

Pascal forcefully distinguishes a philosophically-oriented metaphysical theism from a full-orbed Christian understanding of God as triune and incarnational. One may grant that God exists and not be very moved by that fact, especially if God is regarded merely as performing a few metaphysical functions that fail to impinge on everyday life. On the other hand, a successful theistic argument (of whatever stripe), while falling something short of biblical theism, could move a skeptic or an atheist a bit closer to taking the distinctive claims of religious faith more seriously. For instance, if Jane is argued out of atheism by one or more arguments from natural theology, she may become interested in evaluating the specifically Christian claims about God and Christ found in the Bible. She may even seriously consider Pascal's own arguments concerning the supernatural character of Christ and Scripture (see chapter ten). When she was an atheist, Jane would have had less philosophical incentive to investigate Scripture. Natural theology in the Christian tradition has never been regarded as an end in itself, but rather as a prelude to other evidences and arguments pertaining to its creed. Pascal seems to deny this potentially faith-enhancing function.[4]

Not only did Pascal take the object of these metaphysical arguments to be too abstract, he thought the manner of reasoning they employed was too abstract and abstruse to have any significant effect on the one philosophizing.

> The metaphysical proofs for the existence of God are so remote from human reasoning and so involved that they make little impact, and even if they did help some people, it would only be for the moment during which they watched the demonstration, because an hour later they would be afraid they had made a mistake (190/543).

The philosophical debates over theistic arguments can be quite complex, involving the logic of possible worlds, the nature of causation, big bang cosmology, and much more. Nevertheless, if a "metaphysical proof" (say a cosmological or design argument) is deemed more cogent than its denial, one is left with some rational support for theism. These arguments may be complex and difficult, but if they are mastered they should be convincing.

But perhaps not all of these arguments need be intricate and intellectually taxing to be cogent. One may boil down a complex argument to several simple principles that remain convincing. For instance, one impressed by a cosmological argument (that the universe requires a cause and explanation outside itself) may reason that the universe either (1) was created by God, (2) is eternal (beginning-less and God-less), or (3) popped into existence without a cause a finite time ago. One who takes (2) and (3) to be less plausible than (1) has an argument at hand that is not so "remote from human reasoning" as Pascal may have feared.[5]

But Pascal has a further argument. He claims that successful theistic arguments that have nothing to do with the Incarnation would engender pride in those who engage in them. They could lead one to think that a sufficient knowledge of God is available apart from the work of the Mediator. Pride or self-sufficiency is the opposite of the condition Pascal wants to encourage in a religious seeker. The seeker ought to be humble and receptive before God. Therefore, Pascal rejects these arguments as spiritually perilous (see 352/526; 190/543).

Pascal's apologetic method focuses on Christ, not simply on a Creator or Providence. He passionately wants to convince people of their moral and spiritual need for redemption offered by Jesus Christ. In light of this, he worries that natural theology proves a God without Christ, which might undermine the sense of "wretchedness" that he seeks to demonstrate about the human condition. He believes that God must be "hidden" to some degree in order for creatures to feel their spiritual poverty.

The Christian tradition and other religious traditions do teach that pride is a vice that obscures one's need for spiritual redemption. What is not clear is that a good argument for God's existence would necessarily or even likely encourage that kind of pride in someone who accepts theistic arguments. If an argument for a Creator or Designer or Law-Giver were produced and believed, one might well wonder about one's status before this rather formidable being. Rather than fomenting pride, a winning theistic argument may make a human being seem small in comparison to the metaphysical grandeur of God. That might be the first step toward the humility so vital to Pascal's approach to our knowledge of God.[6]

Even the most robust claims made for natural theology in the Christian tradition stop short of claiming that no more needs to be known about God than what reason, experience, and argument can produce. Thomas Aquinas, the famous author of "the five ways" of proving God, argues that divine revelation is required to know that God was a Trinity and that the Incarnation occurred. Most believers, he claims, will need to believe in God on the basis of the authority of the Bible and the church, since the proofs are not evident to all intellects. Mortimer Adler observes that, "as compared with the thickness of sacred theology, natural theology is very, very thin."[7]

Despite these objections to Pascal's in-principle rejection of natural theology (he never claimed the arguments fail in what they purport to prove), his warnings should remind one that a Christian philosopher interested in making her faith rationally compelling must do more than justify mere monotheism. The intellectual challenge comes in laying out a deeply Christian and logically compelling account of reality, especially concerning the human condition and its remedy.

Instead of arguing for God in abstract terms, Pascal strove to show us who we are in relation to the Creator. He chastised "the philosophers" who neglected the urgent realities of the human condition: "All very well to cry out to a man who does not know himself that he should make his own way to God!" (141/509). Nonetheless, Pascal's complaints about natural theology did not lead him to abandon rationality in favor of a blind leap of faith in the dark.

---

[1] See Stephen T. Davis, *God, Reason, and Theistic Proofs* (Grand Rapids, MI: Eerdmans, 1997) for an excellent and thorough treatment.

[2] Some suggest that the germ of natural theology can be found in biblical passages such as Romans 1 and Acts 17.

[3] See Douglas Groothuis, "Pascal's Biblical Omission Argument Against Natural Theology," *Asbury Theological Journal* 52, no. 2 (Fall 1997): 17-26.

[4] See, Douglas Groothuis, "Do Theistic Proofs Prove the Wrong God?" *Christian Scholar's Review* XXIX:2 (Winter 1999): 247-260.

[5] See Douglas Groothuis, "Are Theistic Arguments Religiously Useless? A Pascalian Objection Examined," *Trinity Journal* (new series) 15 (1994): 147-161.

[6] See Douglas Groothuis, "Proofs, Pride, and Incarnation: Is Natural Theology Theologically Taboo?" *Journal of the Evangelical Theological Society* 38, no. 1 (March 1995): 67-77.

[7] Mortimer Adler, *How To Think About God* (New York: MacMillan Publishing Co., Inc., 1980), 154.

7

Skepticism and the Hidden God

In rejecting natural theology, Pascal walked a philosophical tightrope stretched between the dangers of skepticism and dogmatism. Although his apologetic did not rely on the old theistic proofs, nor Descartes' newer versions of these proofs, Pascal, refused to disable reason as a guide to religious truth. That would have ended apologetics. He was working without a net and faced the challenge with style. Pascal aimed to spark a philosophical and existential crisis in his readers that would be resolvable only by Christian revelation. Many fragments portray this:

> If I saw no sign [in nature] of Divinity I should decide on a negative solution: if I saw signs of a Creator everywhere I should peacefully settle down in faith. But, seeing too much to deny and not enough to affirm, I am in a pitiful state, where I have wished a hundred times over that, if there is a God supporting nature, she should unequivocally proclaim him, and that, if the signs in nature are deceptive, they should be completely erased; that nature should say all or nothing so that I could see what course I ought to follow (429/229).

Pascal's Use of Skepticism

This lamentation, which would have been spoken by an interlocutor in the *Apology*, displays Pascal's use of skepticism: a philosophy that brings knowledge claims into serious question.

50

Skepticism may assault sensory perception, moral values, or the broader meaning of life, including religion. Pascal touches on all three areas. However, his purpose is not destructive, but constructive. Pascal wants us to understand our intellectual weaknesses before a perplexing universe—as is evident from his reflections on "the disproportion of man" (199/72). He believes that humanity's fall into sin has cognitive as well as moral and spiritual ramifications. Pascal sometimes puts this in extreme terms:

> Ecclesiastes shows that man without God is totally ignorant and inescapably unhappy, for anyone is unhappy who wills but cannot do. Now he wants to be happy and assured of some truth, and yet he is equally incapable of knowing and of not desiring to know. He cannot even doubt (75/389).

If Pascal pushes skepticism too far, he will end up in cahoots with essayist Michel Montaigne (1533-92), the influential French arch-skeptic who denied the power of reason to determine truth and who, therefore, only held to religion for purely conventional reasons. Pascal appreciates Montaigne's humbling of "proud reason" (the domain of dogmatism and Descartes), but rejects his terminal skepticism and religious conformity. Pascal opposes the calm and worldly skepticism of French high society, deeming it an enemy of true religion, which calls a person to seek God fervently. Pyrrhonism was a particularly noxious brand of skepticism, according to Pascal. It teaches that one cannot intellectually resolve matters of ultimate consequence since equally good arguments seem to be found on both sides of all issues. Therefore, one should adopt the attitude of ataraxia (philosophical equanimity) in the face of intellectual irresolution.

Pascal, by contrast, advances skepticism as a prelude to faith. Skepticism should not be quickly banished by a few rational moves, in the manner of Descartes. That method does not take human corruption seriously enough. But neither will Pascal reduce reasoning to no better—and sometimes worse—than animal behavior, as did Montaigne. Rather, he exults in human reasoning.

> It is not in space that I must seek my human dignity, but in the ordering of my thought. It will do me no good to own land. Through space the universe grasps me and swallows me up like a speck; through thought I grasp it (113/348).

Skepticism and the Hidden God

In this, Pascal agrees with Descartes: there is a metaphysical difference between matter and mind; or, as Pascal puts it, these are two distinct "orders," which are irreducible to one another metaphysically or axiologically (with respect to value). "Grasping the universe," in a sense, puts both the universe and humans in their rightful places.

> Man is obviously made for thinking. Therein lies all his dignity and his merit; and his whole duty is to think as he ought. Now the order of things is to begin without ourselves, and with our author and our end (620/146; see also 759/346).

Thought, though great, often goes astray; and certainty on matters of ultimate concern is not easily found. Our dignity has been debased.

> Thought, then, is admirable and incomparable by its very nature. It must have had strange faults to have become worthy of contempt, but it does have such faults that nothing is more ridiculous. How great by its nature, how vile by its faults! (756/365).

We thus can understand Pascal's disparaging comments about "philosophy." He is not disparaging reasoning *per se*, but pointing out the limits of philosophizing "under the sun" and apart from divine revelation: "For the philosophers there are 280 different kinds of sovereign good" (479/746; see also 76/73). Pascal's finished *Apology* would have likely surveyed the major philosophical options pertaining to the sovereign good. We are left with poignant suggestions, and perhaps the eerie sense that Pascal is on to something: Do we need to know more than we can know when left only to ourselves? A fragment alludes to Pascal composing a "letter to induce men to seek God. Then make them look for him among the philosophers, sceptics, and dogmatists, who will worry the man who seeks" (4/184).

Descartes wrestled the skeptical demon down with a far different strategy. By methodologically doubting everything possible, he struck bedrock with his statement, "I think, therefore, I am" (*cogito ergo sum*). He cannot be mistaken that he thinks; if he thinks, he must exist. From this, he builds his system, which includes deductive arguments for God's existence and the reality of the external world. These arguments dispense with skepticism and argue for a God who is an abstract and metaphysical being with no organic connection to the Christian Scriptures. Pascal, however, never argues for a generic God, but the specifically Christian God revealed through Christ.

The Hidden God

Skepticism is not the final condition: all is not up for grabs. It is not a resting place, but a launching pad. "We have an incapacity for proving anything which no amount of dogmatism can overcome. We have an idea of truth which no amount of skepticism can overcome" (406/395). Pascal relates this tension to our knowledge of God. God, he claims, is "hidden" in some ways. God is not an item of simple sensory observation or an obvious concept such as one would find in a proof of geometry.

Pascal has some scriptural support for this view. The psalmist exclaims, "But I cry to you for help, O LORD; in the morning my prayer comes before you. Why O LORD, do you reject me and hide your face from me?" (Psalm 88:13-14). The prophet Isaiah also speaks of God as powerful and provident, yet sometimes hidden (Isaiah 45:15). Pascal understands this paradoxical presence and absence as calibrated to the human condition:

> If there were no obscurity [concerning God] man would not feel his corruption; if there were no light man could not hope for a cure. Thus it is not only right but useful for us that God should be partly concealed and partly revealed, since it is equally dangerous for man to know God without knowing his own wretchedness as to know his own wretchedness without knowing God (446/586).

> What can be seen on earth indicates neither the total absence, nor the manifest presence of divinity, but the presence of a hidden God. Everything bears this stamp (449/556).

If God were perfectly obvious to everyone, people could not feel their inadequacies and need for grace and redemption. On the other hand, if there were no signs of deity, there could be no reason to hope for grace and redemption. So God's existence is intimated and suggested in creation, but the divine reality is not overwhelmingly obvious to everyone. Pascal must have realized that in the first chapter of Romans, the Apostle Paul claims that God has revealed himself in creation such that everyone is without excuse if they fail to recognize their Creator. Pascal would, I believe, agree. What he is claiming, along with Paul, is that humans, given their congenitally flawed condition, also tend to deny and suppress the truth revealed in creation. God allows us to shut our ears and turn our eyes away from the divine dimension. Paul says that God chose to create the world and providentially oversee it "so that people would seek him and perhaps reach out for him and find him, though he is not far from each one of us" (Acts 17:27).

Pascal should be quoted at some length to make his extraordinary claim concerning religious knowledge.

> If [God] had wished to overcome the obstinacy of the most hardened, he could have done so by revealing himself to them so plainly that they could not doubt the truth of his essence, as he will appear on the last day. . . .This is not the way he wished to appear when he came in mildness, because so many men had shown themselves unworthy of his clemency, that he wished to deprive them of the good they did not desire. It was therefore not right that he should appear in a manner divine and absolutely capable of convincing all men, but neither was it right that his coming should be so hidden that he could not be recognized by those who sincerely sought him. He wished to make himself perfectly recognizable to them. Thus wishing to appear openly to those who seek him with all their heart and hidden from those who shun him with all their heart, he has qualified our knowledge of him by giving signs which can be seen by those who seek him and not by those who do not.
>
> 'There is enough light for those who desire only to see, and enough darkness for those of a contrary disposition' (149/430).

What Pascal takes to be true for those who encountered Jesus in the flesh, he applies to anyone today who is willing to follow up on the clues God has left in creation for those who seek truth.

The doctrine of the hiddenness of God has generated a significant amount of philosophical discussion recently—pro and con.[1] Rather than canvass this literature, I will interact briefly with Friedrich Nietzsche. Nietzsche finds the notion of a hidden God inconsistent with a God who holds us accountable for our unbelief. If we are left without certainty, how can God rightly regard unbelief as sin?

Skepticism and the Hidden God

A god who is all-knowing and all-powerful and who does not even make sure that his creatures understand his intention— could that be a god of goodness? Who allows countless doubts and dubieties to persist, for thousands of years, as though the salvation of mankind were unaffected by them, and who on the other hand holds out the prospect of frightful consequences if any mistake is made as to the nature of truth?[2]

Nietzsche finds this notion so ridiculous that he excoriates this god as pathetic and miserable, given his limited communication skills. He is like "a deaf and dumb man making all kinds of ambiguous signs when the most fearful danger is about to fall on his child or his dog."[3]

Thinking he has dispensed with this "hidden God," Nietzsche then characteristically engages in psychological genealogy, alleging that the idea originates with "an early, immature intellectuality in man," which "takes lightly the duty to tell the truth" and "as yet know[s] nothing of a duty of God to be truthful toward mankind and clear in the manner of his communications."[4] He esteems Pascal as being the most eloquent spokesperson for this view of God, but explains this by asserting that Pascal "was never able to calm his mind on this matter" because he sensed "a piece of immorality in the 'deus absconditus' [hidden God] and was very fearful and ashamed of admitting it to himself."[5]

Nietzsche's post-theistic autopsy of Pascal's argument is only instructive if the idea of the hidden God is as incoherent as Nietzsche makes it. If not, his impugning of Pascal's motives is *ad hominem* and begs the question. Nietzsche's objection seems to labor under a false assumption. For God to be good and omnipotent, he must reveal himself so clearly as to leave no doubt for all humans, irrespective of their moral condition or attentiveness. But Pascal argues at length that God is available to those who seek him in light of their own intellectual and moral needs. God has left enough clues to make the search warranted.

> As far as the choices go, you must take the trouble to seek the truth, for if you die without worshipping the true principle you are lost. 'But', you say 'if he had wanted me to worship him, he would have left me some signs of his will.' So he did, but you pay no heed. Look for them; it is well worth it (158/236).

Pascal here stresses both the prudential factor—"it is well worth

55

it"—and the epistemic factor of signs being available. One significant sign is the enigma of humanity itself, which is described and explained by the doctrines of creation and the fall. Other signs include religious experience and the uniqueness of Jesus and the Bible.

But one must seek God. Pascal operates under the assumption of what could be called "conditioned cognitive access." Some cognitive claims are only knowable by engaging in certain activities pursuant to their discovery. Access to the knowledge is conditioned by the behavior and personal status of the knower. This knowledge is reserved for those who properly prepare, investigate, and participate.[6]

Consider psychologist Abraham Maslow's comparison of the interpersonal, psychotherapeutic relationship with "spectator knowledge." For the latter, "the nature and uniqueness of the observer is not a great problem. Any competent observer is as good as any other and will see the same truths."[7] A morally debased scientist, if properly trained, can use a radio telescope just as skillfully as a morally upright astronomer. But in the case of the interpersonal relationship, "The nature of the knower is a *sine qua non* of the nature of the known. Knowers are not easily interchangeable."[8] An unsympathetic therapist will know less about a patient than one who sympathetically approaches the patient as an important human being. The personal dynamic is epistemically relevant in this context, as well as in many others. Conditioned epistemic access is involved in this acquisition of knowledge.

Of course, even an unsympathetic therapist knows her client exists. This differs from the person who wonders whether or not God exists. Nevertheless, certain actions and attitudes are necessary for pursuing the matter of God successfully. The orientation of the knower is not inconsequential. The detective who is passionately concerned to find his lost son—who may be dead or alive—is more likely to sniff out every lead and follow up every clue than is the dispassionate police agent assigned to the case by his superior. Pascal wants to kindle this detective-father kind of passion to seek out God, even if God is not yet squarely within our sights.

Pascal might retort to Nietzsche: "You are laboring under a false premise, Professor. The knowledge of God is not an impersonal commodity abstractly dispensed. It is dependent upon the condition of the knower, because God is a personal and moral being who desires to enter into a relationship with his creatures through the Incarnation. A certain rapport or respect must be established for the knowledge to be possible. But even if this occurs, it is by God's efficacious grace."[9]

Nietzsche, it seems, had no patience with the kind of humility that Pascal recommended. (Or, he may have had it and later lost it.) His rejection of theism appears as much dispositional as philosophical. God must die so the Superman, or Overman (Nietzsche's ideal human, who is free from God and the dictates of "the herd"), can live and thrive. Consider this statement concerning God by "the ugliest man" from *Thus Spoke Zarathustra:*

> But he had to die: he saw with eyes that saw everything; he saw man's depths and ultimate grounds, all his concealed disgrace and ugliness. His pity knew no shame: he crawled into my dirtiest nooks. This most curious, overobtrusive one had to die. He always saw me: on such a witness I wanted to have my revenge or not live myself. The god who saw everything, even man—this god had to die! Man cannot bear it that such a witness should live.[10]

Zarathustra, presumably speaking for Nietzsche, approves of the speech. But the statement is not a rational argument against God's existence; it is an outright revulsion at the thought of omniscience. It defies as much as it denies. Nietzsche would not be expected to have attained a personal knowledge of God in light of his resolute hostility. Nor would an apathetic or indifferent person attain such knowledge.

A critic might say that this proposal of "conditioned cognitive access" simply begs the question. It assumes that there is a God with a particular character, and it assumes that humans are so corrupted that they must seek God if he is to be found. Thus no real argument is given, but only a religious exhortation.

On the contrary, many knowledge claims have built-in conditions which must be satisfied for the particular knowledge to be disclosed. They do not beg any questions, but rather stipulate conditions under which certain kinds of knowledge may be attained. One cannot know, or reasonably believe, some things in isolation from a specific process or regimen. This is true in psychology and in other human relationships. I will again take up the idea of pursuing beliefs in discussing Pascal's wager argument, but for now I suggest that Pascal's claim is not incoherent or irrational, but quite plausible.

Christian philosopher C. S. Lewis also addressed the question of divine obscurity in an essay called "Dogma and the Universe." Since God must transcend what finite and contingent beings can conceive, it "is to be expected that His creation should be, in the main, unintelligible to us."[11]

I suspect that there is something in our very mode of thought which makes it inevitable that we should always be baffled by actual existence, whatever character actual existence may have. Perhaps a finite and contingent creature—a creature that might not have existed—will always find it hard to acquiesce in the brute fact that it is, here and now, attached to an actual order of things.[12]

Pascal writes of this sense of cosmic wonder when he is describing the plight of "the wretchedness of man without God."

Why have limits been set upon my knowledge, my height, my life, making it a hundred rather than a thousand years? For what reason did nature make it so, and choose this rather than that mean from the whole of infinity, when there is no more reason to choose one rather than another, as none is more attractive than another? (194/208).

Finite beings conscious of their contingency might be baffled or puzzled by just about any logically possible universe. To be finite is, in some sense, to be deprived of some things; only the infinite is all-encompassing. Therefore, the fact of cosmic bafflement should not decisively count against God. But bafflement, argues Pascal, ought not engender apathy, but rather a serious quest for God.

Against Indifference

As a philosophical irritant, Pascal marshaled a battery of considerations against those who were indifferent to their ignorance and who simply did not care whether or not God existed. A modern example of the attitude Pascal targeted is found in Roger Scruton's *Modern Philosophy*. In discussing skepticism, Scruton calmly asserts:

Some beliefs are, so to speak, epistemological luxuries. I could give them up without losing my conceptions of the world and my place within it. Consider the belief in God; it may be morally and emotionally difficult for me to abandon this belief. But if the sceptic showed that I could not conceivably have any grounds for it, he would not undermine my conception of the world.[13]

Not surprisingly, Scruton's large volume contains no reference to Pascal in its index. Although Scruton grants some moral or emotional distress at the prospect of losing God, he evinces no deep concern over the prospect of a godless universe. Apparently, he thinks that little follows from the divine absence.

Pascal denounces indifference toward religion as violating the principles of reasonable self-interest. Here he narrates the speech of a skeptic who expresses his utter lostness in the cosmos:

> Just as I do not know whence I come, so I do not know whither I am going. All I know is that when I leave this world I shall fall forever into nothingness or into the hands of a wrathful God, but I do not know which of these two states is to be my eternal lot. Such is my state, full of weakness and uncertainty. And my conclusion from all this is that I must pass my days without a thought of seeking what is to happen to me. Perhaps I might find some enlightenment in my doubts, but I do not want to take the trouble... (427/194)

At this statement, Pascal issues four red-hot questions.

> Who would wish to have as a friend a man who argued like that? Who would choose him from among others as a confidant in his affairs? Who would resort to him in adversity? To what use in life could he possibly be turned? (427/194)

These questions are not mere *ad hominem* attacks; they form an argument. If it is a good thing to be a trustworthy friend, and if such a friend would never be as nonchalant about his destiny as is the skeptic, then it is not a good thing to be a negligent, skeptical person. This kind of skeptic has failed to discharge a basic human duty to investigate matters of extreme moment.

In confronting this intellectual indolence, Pascal is as much an existential therapist as a philosopher. He realizes that he must treat such worldly complacency with explosives by stimulating the imagination, as in this memorable parable.

> A man in a dungeon, not knowing whether sentence has been

passed on to him, with only an hour left to find out, and that hour enough, once he knows it has been passed, to have it revoked. It would be unnatural for him to spend that hour not finding out whether sentence has been passed by playing piquet (163/200).

Pascal challenges us to face our mortality. But unlike Martin Heidegger, who in his *Being and Time* saw humanity's "being unto death" as a call to live authentically for a *finite* period of time, Pascal wants to spark a hope for transcendence, for an *infinite* life conferred by God, for a way out at the end.

Why should one seek? Pascal believes that the Christian perspective is "worthy of reverence because it really understands human nature" (12/17). We examine Pascal's provocative case for this next.

---

[1] See John O'Leary-Hawthorn, "Arguments for Atheism," in *Reason for the Hope Within*, ed. Michael J. Murphy, (Grand Rapids, MI: William B. Eerdmans Publishing Company, 1999), 122-124.

[2] Friedrich Nietzsche, *Daybreak*, trans. R. J. Hollingdale (Cambridge: Cambridge University Press, 1985), 52.

[3] Ibid., 53.

[4] Ibid.

[5] Ibid.

[6] See C. Stephen Evans, *Philosophy of Religion* (Downers Grove, IL: InterVarsity Press, 1985), 174.

[7] Abraham Maslow, *The Psychology of Science* (New York: Harper and Row, 1966), 105.

[8] Ibid.

[9] In his meditation, "The Mystery of Jesus," Pascal has Jesus say, "Take comfort; you would not seek me if you had not found me" (919/553), thus implying that those who truly seek are already the objects of saving grace. This fits with his theological compatiblism. See chapter four on this.

[10] Friedrich Nietzsche, *Thus Spoke Zarathustra*, in *The Portable Nietzsche*, ed. Walter Kaufmann (New York: The Viking Press, 1975), 379.

[11] C. S. Lewis, *God in the Dock* (Grand Rapids, MI: Eerdmans, 1970), 43.

[12] Ibid., 40.

[13] Roger Scruton, *Modern Philosophy* (New York: Penguin, 1994), 17.

8

Deposed Royalty

The Bible is God's anthropology rather than man's theology—
Abraham Heschel.[1]

In *Walden*, Henry David Thoreau observed that "the majority of
men lead lives of quiet desperation"—or not such quiet desperation, we
might add today, given cell phones, beepers, pagers, and especially
subwoofers. Pascal would agree with Thoreau and go on to claim that
despite being "east of Eden," humans are not irreparably estranged
from their true good or home. He attempts to explain the human enigma
and to offer the tonic of Christian faith. Pascal's rejection of natural
theology does not hinder his efforts to give persuasive arguments in
favor of Christianity. He develops several philosophical strategies,
including an argument from human nature in support of Christian
revelation. He argues that Christian doctrines best explain the
paradoxes of the human condition and render Christianity worthy of
respect.

Human Greatness and Misery

The true religion, Pascal argues, must be able to explain the
human condition better than its rivals. "Man's greatness and
wretchedness are so evident that the true religion must necessarily
teach us that there is in man some great principle of greatness and some
great principle of wretchedness" (149/430). Humans are a curious
mixture of widely divergent properties. Science and technology had
made tremendous progress in Pascal's day, much of it at his hand; yet
truth often escapes the ingenious inventors. Pascal exclaims:

61

> What sort of freak then is man! How novel, how monstrous, how chaotic, how paradoxical, how prodigious! Judge of all things, feeble earthworm, repository of truth, sink of doubt and error, the glory and refuse of the universe! (131/434).

Pascal presses the incongruous juxtapositions of human life throughout the *Pensées*. He does not simply affirm the variety of human experiences, but underscores the painful condition of being situated between total skepticism and dogmatic assurance. Many of the fragments of *Pensées* discuss the ironies and absurdities of this juxtaposition. This serves Pascal's purpose of showing from nature that nature is corrupt, as he puts it (6/60). He explores the human condition in such a way as to suggest that it is a flawed version of an earlier model.

Pascal does not reject reason, experimentation or observation as vain or arrogant in all cases; yet he sees human finitude and cognitive corruption as severely circumscribing the powers of autonomous reason. He affirms that thought exalts humans over nature and that "all [human] dignity consists in thought" (200/347). Pascal also speaks of the fragility of reason, its lack of stamina in the face of external distractions. Though it confers dignity upon humanity, reason is easily thrown off course. We are always subject to nature's ways of disorienting and even eradicating us: "a vapor, a drop of water is enough to kill" us (200/347).

Pascal makes much of this vulnerability in relation to his argument that humans are fallen creatures. This is the doctrine of "original sin." Humans were once naturally in concord with themselves, others, nature, and God. Yet through moral transgression against God, humans were banished from such harmonious arrangements and suffered a constitutional corruption that involves everyone (spare Jesus Christ, who is sinless) and continues down through the ages and today. Although Pascal believed in a literal first human couple specially created by God through a direct supernatural act (see Genesis 1 and 2), his insights about the fall of humanity can be accommodated and conserved by less literal interpretations.[2] Pascal's primary point is that the first humans (however God brought them about) transgressed the divine way of life and love, fell from grace into corruption, and this corruption has been passed down to successive generations, who, in turn, experience the same alienation, fragmentation and disharmony set forth in the third chapter of Genesis.

All of our capacities have thus been defaced, yet not entirely erased. We can conceive of their perfection but must endure their inadequacies. Even the normal operations of human reason are easily derailed by factors beyond our control.

> The mind of this supreme judge of the world [i.e., man] is not so independent as to be impervious to whatever din may be going on near by. . . . Do not be surprised if his reasoning is not too sound at the moment, there is a fly buzzing round his ears; that is enough to render him incapable of giving good advice (48/366).

This observation does not undermine the capacity of reason to discern truth any more than inclement weather undermines the ability of a jet aircraft to fly. It simply situates reason within the confines of human "wretchedness" and calls humans to contemplate this limitation.

Pascal considers in various fragments the tendency of human thought toward presumption (what he calls "proud reason"— pretentious and thus unreasonable), as well as distortion through unruly passions and imagination.

> Man is obviously made for thinking. Therein lies all his dignity and his merit; and his whole duty is to think as he ought. Now the order of thought is to begin with ourselves, and with our author and our end. Now what does the world think about? Never about that, but about dancing, playing the lute, singing, writing verse, tilting at the ring, etc., and fighting, becoming king, without thinking what it means to be a king or to be a man (620/146).

Those crowned with dignity and honor misuse the very faculty that dignifies them; they divert their attention from ultimate matters through their infatuation with the mundane and the trivial. Their greatness is abused, yet still in evidence. The very awareness of wretchedness bespeaks greatness. "Man's greatness comes from knowing he is wretched: a tree does not know it is wretched. Thus it is wretched to know that one is wretched, but there is a greatness in knowing one is wretched" (114/397). For Pascal, the recognition of human limitation is a sign of excellence, because it reveals a self-consciousness unknown in the nonhuman realm. Even some moral failings reveal a kind of ingenuity that inspires admiration: "Man's greatness even in his concupiscence. He has managed to produce such a

63

remarkable system from it and make it the image of true charity" (118/402; see also 106/403).

Pascal does not give any examples of what he means, but an example from the incorrigible Rousseau is *apropos*. Historian Paul Johnson notes that Jean Jacques Rousseau's rhetorical prowess was often employed deceitfully for self-justifying endeavors. Rousseau believed that his level of genius demanded that the world provide him a living. To this end, he would sponge off various wealthy patrons until they found him intolerable and sent the pouting philosopher packing.

> Rousseau marked most of his major quarrels by composing a gigantic letter of remonstrance. These documents are among his most brilliant works, miracles of forensic skill in which evidence is cunningly fabricated, history rewritten and chronology confused with superb ingenuity in order to prove that the recipient is a monster.[3]

Rousseau showed intellectual greatness even in his concupiscence (in this case, excessive self-love). He would have been an effective manager of political campaigns today.

Despite the greatness of human reason, the opportunities and modalities for deception are legion. Human reasoning is intrinsically debilitated through the fall (45/83). It is thus hindered by a multitude of factors that frustrate its aims: imagination, illness, self-interest, diversion, misperception, custom, pride, vanity, contrariety (conflicting propensities), the follies of science and philosophy, and human injustice. Human reason, according to Pascal, has always been limited in that humans are incorrigibly finite knowers who must depend upon God's revelation for knowledge concerning matters of ultimate concern. This was true even in humanity's unfallen, Edenic estate. However, since the fall, humans do not naturally position themselves as finite knowers epistemically dependent on God as revelator. Rather, they confidently attempt to know the universe autonomously, or they pessimistically succumb to utter skepticism.

Pascal's reflections on greatness and wretchedness are part of an anthropology that appeals to the common facts of human experience, not to the Christian Scriptures. His direct appeal to the Bible comes in the second part of the *Apology*: "There is a Redeemer, proved by Scripture" (6/60). Pascal's anthropology is designed not to yield a systematic and scientific assessment, but to force an anthropological crisis, and to point out that humans, when carefully considered, are mysteries even to themselves. "Man is neither angel nor beast, and it is unfortunately the case that anyone attempting to act as an angel ends up as a beast" (678/358). Pascal outlines how he desires to foment an anthropological crisis in this fragment.

> If he exalts himself, I humble him.
> If he humbles himself, I exalt him.
> And I go on contradicting him
> Until he understands
> That he is a monster that passes all understanding (130/420).

No Consolation from Philosophy

Pascal maintains that merely human philosophies are unable to tell us who we are because they fall into two equal and opposite errors concerning humanity. Either they exalt greatness at the expense of wretchedness or they exalt wretchedness at the expense of greatness. This is brought out clearly in the document that narrates a discussion between Pascal and Monsieur De Sacy (a spiritual leader at Port-Royal des Champes) on the uses of philosophy in the service of Christian faith.

The two representative philosophers are Epictetus (c.55-135) and Michel Montaigne (1533-1592), each of whom is admirable in one dimension but imbalanced overall. Epictetus, the Stoic, understands the duties of human beings, the importance of obedience to God, and the virtue of humility. Nevertheless, Epictetus errs in thinking that people can live up to the standards he lays down, and so falls into a wicked pride that leads him to believe that the soul is divine and suicide is permissible in some cases.[4]

Montaigne, conversely, is a skeptic and a tonic for "haughty reason." His extended reflections on human ignorance and the quandaries of reason deflate the hollow rationalism of the excessively confident. Pascal confesses his joy that Montaigne uses "haughty reason" against itself to reveal its own insufficiencies.[5] Yet Montaigne advises that in the face of skeptical considerations, we remain uncommitted and refuse to search for unattainable truth and goodness.

Each system of thought contains a truth denied by the other. Stoicism conserves greatness and rejects wretchedness, thus lapsing into presumption and pride. Skepticism conserves wretchedness and rejects greatness, thus lapsing into truth-less resignation. Even though it appears that "you would have a perfect morality by binding [the two systems] together,"[6] they cannot be synthesized by selecting compatible elements from each system. This is because Stoicism promotes certainty, while skepticism promotes doubt; Stoicism argues for the greatness of humanity, and skepticism argues for the weakness of humanity. Given this incompatibility, each system would "destroy both the truth and the false position of the other."[7] "Thus they can neither stand alone because of their faults, nor unite because of their differences, and in so doing [they] wreck and annihilate each other to leave the way open for the truth of the Gospel."[8]

Pascal's anthropology does not exhaust the philosophical options, but calls into question two views that were very appealing to those in seventeenth century France who were rediscovering classical philosophy. Variations of these views are with us today. Pascal's argument is twofold. First, neither view fully accounts for the human condition as one of both misery and greatness in both the ethical and epistemic dimensions. Second, a synthesis of the pagan views is not possible either, thus excluding another purely philosophical move. Pascal offers a *tertium quid*. He opens up the discourse to an explanation that transcends any human philosophical system—one that is beyond, but not against, unaided reason.[9] "Reason's last step is the recognition that there are an infinite number of things which are beyond it" (188/267).

According to Pascal, the Gospel harmonizes the contradictions "by a wholly divine skill"[10] that unites the respective truths and expels all falsehood; it thus creates "a truly celestial wisdom in which opposites, incompatible in human doctrines, agree."[11] The philosophers wrongly place contrary descriptions on the same subject; one philosophy says that human nature is great; the other says that it is wretched. However, both predicates cannot obtain of the same subject universally. Yet biblical revelation tells us that we should attribute all wretchedness to our fallen nature and all that is great to grace. (Pascal says in *Pensées* that human greatness is dimly felt as our original nature.) This is the innovation that only God could teach. We need not attribute contradictory predicates to the same subject. Humans have a *dual nature* of a kind not proposed by the philosophers. Humans have fallen from a previous state that is now unattainable, but which is yet recognizable even in the ruins of humanity. We are not completely corrupted; we are not purely great. Neither do we have two souls: one good, one evil.

> Man's dualism is so obvious that some people have thought he had two souls: Because a simple being seemed to them incapable

of such great and sudden variations, from boundless presumption to appalling dejection (629/417).

This contradictory state of affairs has "amazed all mankind, and split them into such different schools of thought" (149/430). There is something deeply mysterious about human nature if it is capable of generating so many diverse—and sometimes logically incompatible—interpretations by philosophers. Although we seldom puzzle over the behavior of pets, though they might amuse us, we often find other people's actions to be unexpected if not indecipherable. A best friend may risk his life for you only to betray you for personal advantage down the road. What accounts for such "contradictions"?

Instead of arguing for a general theism through natural theology, he invokes the Christian worldview in order to account for and give meaning to the human condition. The form of argument is neither inductive nor deductive but abductive. It is an appeal to a compelling explanation, a postulate that illuminates material not otherwise as intelligible or as significant. Philosopher C.S. Peirce explained it this way: "The surprising fact, C, is observed. But if A were true, C would be a matter of course. Hence, there is reason to suspect that A is true."[12] The "surprising fact," for Pascal, is the contradictory nature of humanity. What renders this condition a "matter of course" is humanity's fall from greatness. We are deposed royalty vainly seeking a lost throne beyond our failing, mortal grasp.

Abductive argument is often used in scientific theorizing and in courts of law. If astrophysicists are attempting to explain the origin of the moon or some other satellite or planet, they cannot conduct inductive experimentation to repeat the original process. Neither is deduction available. Instead, they attempt to survey the available data about the moon and its surroundings and postulate an explanation for its existence and nature. In court, various kinds of evidence are arrayed in support of a judgment concerning the guilt or innocence of the party on trial. A person accused of larceny must give a better explanation of his whereabouts during the crime in question than does the prosecutor.

In making this abductive argument, Pascal appeals to a wide variety of relevant anthropological confirmations. If we grant the theological concepts of creation and fall, the human landscape is illuminated to a greater degree than if we deny them. To delineate the theological notion of the fall, Pascal narrates from God's perspective:

'But you are no longer in the state in which I made you. I

67

created man holy, innocent, perfect, I filled him with light and understanding, I showed him my glory and my wondrous works. Man's eye then beheld the majesty of God. He was not then in the darkness that now blinds his sight, nor subject to death and the miseries that afflict him.

'But he could not bear such great glory without falling to presumption. He wanted to make himself his own centre and do without my help. He withdrew himself from my rule, setting himself up as my equal in his desire to find happiness in himself, and I abandoned him to himself. The creatures who were subject to him I incited to revolt and made his enemies, so that today man has become like the beasts, and is so far apart from me that a barely glimmering idea of his author alone remains of all his dead or flickering knowledge (149/430).

Humans retaining some "feeble instinct from the happiness of their first nature" despite their "wretchedness and concupiscence, which has become their second nature" (149/430). This dual nature explains the contradictions that the philosophers could not reconcile.

We can liken the human condition to the present batting swing of a Reggie Jackson (b. 1946). The odds are that even years after retiring from baseball, his swing is still smooth and crisp—although incapable of hitting major league pitching. To say that Reggie was always in his present state is to emphasize misery at the expense of greatness; to say that he is still his prime is to emphasize greatness at the expense of misery. In the case of Jackson we have more than a dim recollection of former greatness; it is a matter of verifiable fact. The case for human fallenness cannot be verified historically (apart from the biblical texts). It is, rather, a theological postulate or hypothesis used to explain historical phenomena. Pascal stipulates that the true religion must explain human nature if it is to be credible, and all religions address the human condition. The reason for greatness is the original, unfallen state; the principle of wretchedness is the fall into sin.

Seeing the fall as an explanation for a perplexing situation, Pascal enlists a principle that accords with his notion of humans having lost a former glory: namely, the principle that we cannot miss what we never had. Our present state of corruption is only miserable because of a previous incorruption enjoyed by the species. He says:

The point is that if man had never been corrupted, he would, in his innocence, confidently enjoy both truth and felicity, and, if man had never been anything but corrupt, he would have no idea either of truth or bliss. But unhappy as we are (and we should be less so if there were no element of greatness in our condition) we have an idea of happiness but we cannot attain it. We perceive an image of the truth and possess nothing but falsehood (131/434).

All these examples of wretchedness prove his greatness. It is the wretchedness of a great lord, the wretchedness of a dispossessed king (116/398).

Pascal further asks, "Who would indeed think himself unhappy not to be king except one who had been dispossessed?" (117/409). No one, he avers, is unhappy because he has but one mouth; but someone with only one eye is unhappy. No one is distressed at not having three eyes, but those with none suffer greatly. Unhappiness comes from being deprived of what we are accustomed to having or what is natural to possess.

Pascal's observations concerning the reason for human misery should not be isolated from his total argument on human nature. He is merely emphasizing that people often suffer more acutely from goods lost than from the lack of goods never possessed. He then uses this as an illustration of the truth of his postulate about human fallenness: we retain some inkling of a former state of incorruption, and we suffer over the loss of using our powers perfectly, even if we do not necessarily identify our sense of loss in this manner.

Pursuing the Best Explanation

To defend his anthropological argument, Pascal must support three claims: (1) that the construal of humanity as having a "dual nature" is intellectually cogent; (2) that the human condition even needs to be explained at all; (3) that the explanation provided by the doctrine of original sin is convincing.

First, in order for his argument to get started, Pascal needs to describe the human condition in a way that makes sense. I submit that his analysis of the greatness and wretchedness of humanity rings true, and that this, at least in part, explains the continuing interest in Pascal. He holds before us a mirror that reflects the whole person in its bewildering contrariety. Martin Warner notes that the power of Pascal's

69

fragments on "epistemology, psychology, ethics, politics, the law, and even such matters as choice of career" lies "partly in the precision of observation and partly in their range and scope that provide a cumulative effect." These observations "invite interpretation in terms of man's 'wretchedness' ('misere') or 'greatness' ('grandeur') or, more often, of the tension between the two."[13] Pascal strikes several chords that combine to register uncommon insights into human nature. These varied observations and judgments have a cumulative effect. No one reflection demonstrates the Christian position; but many mutually reinforcing reflections suggest a reevaluation of an irreligious or otherwise non-Christian perspective.

Second, even if we grant that Pascal's description of the human condition is poignant and rings true to experience, the intractable skeptic could simply grant that human life is full of contradictions and conundra that transcend our rational ability to explain them. Why do we need to explain them at all, especially when this involves unverifiable metaphysics? Why should we force an anthropological crisis when life is difficult enough already?

Philosophers and sages throughout the ages have counseled us to know ourselves. While their answers to the question of human nature have drastically differed, the question tenaciously remains. The issue is at the very marrow of our existence, as is highlighted when Socrates queries in the *Phaedrus*: "Am I a monster more complicated and swollen with passion than the serpent Typho, or a creature of simpler, gentler nature, partaking of something divine?"[14] Pascal wants to go beyond the nonchalant skepticism that is content to chronicle human folly and leave it at that. He advances a compelling explanation that is both existentially appealing and rationally credible.

In evaluating "the philosophers," Pascal says that because they "do not know what your true good is, nor what your true state is," they could not "provide cures for ills which they did not even know" (149/430). Ignorance or misunderstanding of one's condition can easily result in poor or even tragic advice, as when a doctor misdiagnoses a condition and then prescribes the wrong treatment for a serious disease he never discerned. Pascal argues that a mere survey of the anthropological and psychological facts is not sufficient. We need to know something of our origin and nature if we are to have any hope of self-understanding, religious insight, spiritual renewal, or moral improvement. We should not remain indifferent, but seek truth.

Pascal also argues on the skeptic's grounds that the diversions into which he would flee are ultimately existentially unsatisfying. They may temporarily distract one from grim realities, but the hollowness within remains. This is why diversion never finally delivers peace or meaning. Although Pascal writes tellingly of "the hidden God," he also argues that people hide from the truth of their own condition and thereby hide from the possibility of finding a remedy. Truth is easy to flee (through diversion), but it may not be easy to find: "Truth is so obscured nowadays and lies so well established that unless we love the truth we shall never recognize it" (739/864; see also 740/583).

Furthermore, Pascal is not describing the human situation as fallen without remedy; his analysis anticipates a solution to the problem through the Incarnation, a doctrine that presupposes and addresses humanity's dual nature. Pascal's aphorism captures this: "Jesus is a God we can approach without pride and before whom we can humble ourselves without despair" (212/528). This prospect of life and hope should further spark one's prudential interest in the issue. There may be hope for restoration. But one must flee diversion to investigate that possibility.

> Diversion prevents us from thinking about ourselves and leads us imperceptibly to destruction. But...[without diversion] we should be bored, and boredom would drive us to seek some more solid means of escape, but diversion passes our time and brings us imperceptibly to our death (414/171).

> We run heedlessly into the abyss after putting something in front of us to stop us [from] seeing it (166/183).

Pascal urges the skeptic to view the world from a different angle in order to see if that view is better able to reconcile conflicting descriptions and to illuminate the human landscape.

> Know then, proud man, what a paradox you are to yourself. Be humble, impotent reason! Be silent, feeble nature! Learn that man infinitely transcends man, hear from your master your true condition, which is unknown to you.
> Listen to God (131/434).

By speaking of human greatness and misery in a number of contexts, Pascal invites us to understand human nature from a different vantage point, to interpret it in a novel way. "Follow your own impulses. Observe yourself, and see if you do not find the living characteristics of these two natures" (149/430).

Suppose you come across a perplexing painting in an art gallery. It is difficult to evaluate aesthetically because it shows marks of brilliance as well as serious defects. As long as you study the painting strictly according to appearances, you remain stymied. Why is there both brilliance and defect? Why would the painter combine such features so oddly? Later a guide in the art gallery informs you that a great master painted this, but that it suffered corruption through mistreatment by thieves. You then begin to see the same painting from a new vantage point. The greatness of the original creation is now clearly revealed (even though you cannot fully see its original greatness), as is the corruption. This vital background information, not deducible from the painting alone, explains the mystery of the painting. One can now see the same picture with new insight and a fuller awareness. Pascal is making a similar claim. To truly understand human nature, humans must see themselves within an ultimately theological framework.[15] They need a divine disclosure.

Pascal faces a third challenge to his anthropological argument. He is not unaware of the difficulties with the doctrine of original sin. He acknowledges these difficulties in an interesting fragment that describes his anthropological angle quite clearly.

> Original sin is folly in the eyes of men, but it is put forward as such. You should not reproach me for the unreasonable nature of this doctrine, because I put it forward as being unreasonable. But the folly is wiser than all men's wisdom, it is wiser than men [1 Cor. 1:25]. For without it, what are we to say man is? His whole state depends on this imperceptible point. How could he have become aware of it through his reason, seeing that it is something contrary to reason and that his reason, far from discovering it by its own methods, draws away when presented with it? (695/445).

Despite the "offensive" quality of this doctrine, Pascal embraces it because of its explanatory power.

> Certainly nothing jolts us more rudely than this doctrine, and yet, but for this mystery, the most incomprehensible of all, we remain incomprehensible to ourselves. The knot of our condition was twisted and turned in that abyss, so that it is harder to conceive of man without this mystery than for man to conceive of it himself (131/434).

The doctrine of original sin may leave us with unanswered questions about why God allowed corruption to enter creation, but it fits the facts as we observe them: humans show signs of being both royal and wretched.

A critic may suggest that one mystery can never explain another; it only multiplies the confusion. To answer this complaint, we can compare Pascal's argument with other kinds of explanatory hypotheses. Consider criminal detective work. Many seemingly inexplicable facts in a crime can be understood once the criminal is identified. When Ted Bundy was found to be guilty of numerous homicides, these homicides were *explained* in some ways. A pattern could be detected in his evil actions. It may be mysterious why an intelligent, attractive, and capable person would become a mass murderer (the greatness and misery issue is also writ large). Nonetheless, many facts can be explained after he is identified as the murderer. Mysteries remain, but mysteries may also explain.

Pascal regards the doctrine of original sin as "beyond reason" (without being illogical) and "an offense to reason" in that it calls human autonomy to account (see 188/267). Yet he deems original sin a mystery that *explains* the puzzle of the human condition. Without this mystery we remain incomprehensible to ourselves, enigmatic monstrosities. But if we long to minimize the mystery, erase the enigma, explain our lot, and find hope for redemption, Pascal claims that we should invoke the Christian categories of creation, fall—and Incarnation. Having come to terms with ourselves as deposed monarchs, we find liberation only through a Mediator. Through Christ, "we know our own wretchedness, because this God is nothing less than our redeemer from wretchedness. Thus we can know God properly only by knowing our own iniquities" (189/547).

An Initial Treatment for Unbelief

Pascal argues that the claim of divine revelation solves the riddle of the human condition by providing a compelling theological explanation to a philosophical and existential conundrum. He throws down the gauntlet after specifying the need to explain the human condition and supply a concrete hope: "Let us examine all the religions of the world on that point and let us see whether any but the Christian religion meets it" (149/430). Pascal did assess some aspects of Islam and had much to say about Judaism in relation to Christianity, but he

73

did not attempt a systematic and comprehensive exercise in comparative anthropology. However, the Christian explanation may be compared with potential rivals on a case-by-case basis.

Pascal never systematically formulated his anthropological argument. Nonetheless, it may challenge one to reflect seriously on its merits. Pascal thought the wager argument would provide a further incentive to belief, as we will see in the next installment.

---

[1] Abraham Heschel, *God in Search of Man: A Philosophy of Judaism* (New York: Farrar, Straus, and Girox, 1976), 412.

[2] Pascal thought that science (the order of the body) could not conflict with supernatural matters received by faith (the order of the heart). One wonders how Pascal would have assessed the later claims by some Darwinists that evolutionary theory undermines the divine origination of humanity. On the contemporary contours of this controversy, see William A. Dembski, ed., *Mere Creation: Science, Faith and Intelligent Design* (Downers Grove, IL: InterVarsity Press, 1998).

[3] Paul Johnson, *Intellectuals* (New York: Harper and Row, 1988), 14.

[4] Blaise Pascal, "Discussion with Monsieur De Sacy," in Blaise Pascal, *Pensées and Other Writings*, trans. Honor Levi; ed. Anthony Levi (New York: Oxford University Press, 1995), 183.

[5] Ibid., 187.

[6] Ibid., 190.

[7] Ibid.

[8] Ibid.

[9] See Pascal, *Pensées*, 173/273; 174/270; 185/265; 188/267.

[10] Pascal, "Discussion," 190.

[11] Ibid.

[12] Charles Peirce, *Collected Papers of Charles Sanders Peirce*, ed. C. Hartshorne and P. Weiss, 6 vols. (Cambridge, MA: Harvard University Press, 1931-35), B, 69a; quoted in Michael Warner, *Philosophical Finesse* (Oxford: Clarendon Press, 1989), 25.

[13] Warner, 176.

[14] Plato, *Phaedrus*, 230a.

[15] See Geddes MacGregor, *Introduction to Religious Philosophy* (Boston: Houghton Mifflin Company, 1959), 142-43. I have changed his illustration somewhat.

9

Wagering a Life on God

Pascal's wager is a well-known and much-debated argument in philosophy. Unlike many philosophical debates, it captures the imagination and triggers strong passions on both sides. Although the essential idea of the wager was not entirely new to Pascal, his concerns as a mathematician who did groundbreaking work in probability theory, as well as his enthusiasm as an avid defender of Christianity, give the wager its psychological and logical bite.

The wager is one of the longer fragments of the *Pensées*. However, unlike the few other longer fragments, it may not have been a finished essay. It was written on four sides of a single folded sheet. Some paragraphs are inserted into the main text, other sentences are written vertically up the margins, and parts are written upside down on the page. Anthony Levi claims that "no matter how the constitutive pieces are arranged, the four sides of manuscript cannot be made to yield a single coherent linear text."[1] Nevertheless, the version we find in modern translations can be divided into four basic sections: prologue, assessment of the stakes and the odds, spiritual experiment, and coda. There is a flow to the argument, however many mysteries remain within it.

Although the fragment was left unclassified by Pascal, several commentators have suggested that the wager would have been the turning point in Pascal's proposed *Apology*. Krailshaimer argues that from "the march and content of the argument" the wager "is most probably intended to come at the hinge of the *Apology*" when "the unbeliever is ready to give Christianity a trial."[2] Pascal's previous arguments would have attempted to make Christianity worth further investigation. His "deposed royalty" argument attempts to make Christianity "worthy of respect" (12/187). To this he now adds a prudential element, which he hopes, will captivate the seeker and

75

compel her to consider other reasons for belief.

Prologue: Agnosticism and God

Pascal first argues for the remoteness of God by virtue of divine infinity. Because "the finite is annihilated in the presence of the infinite" so as to become pure nothingness, a finite human knower cannot know the nature of an infinite God (418/233; subsequent references will refer to this fragment unless noted). We may know that the infinite exists without knowing its nature. Consider "an infinite number": its nature is unknown since it is neither odd nor even, yet we believe that it exists. But God is even more incomprehensible than an infinite number, and it is only by faith that we know his existence. God is "infinitely beyond our comprehension, since being indivisible and without limits, he bears no relation to us."[3] Therefore, we are "incapable of knowing either what he is or whether he is."

Pascal then defends Christians for not claiming that reason can establish the existence or nature of God, since it is impossible given the very notion of God's infinity. Nevertheless, the coin falls only one of two ways. Either God is, or he is not, but "reason cannot make you choose either, reason cannot prove either wrong." Then Pascal urges his interlocutor to bet on God and lays out the odds and the stakes.

Pascal's prologue seems to imply a terminal agnosticism. The logical choice is a simple case of either/or: God is or God is not. But no final "proof" can be given on either side. We are thus at an absolute impasse. Pascal may have wanted to entice the most hardened skeptic here, one who would not have found his anthropological argument compelling or even suggestive. In this case, he would be granting a premise for the sake of argument, which he himself does not hold. But such a strategy is hazardous philosophically.

If God bears *no* relation to us, we are at a loss to describe God at all. No divine attributes would be knowable if God were "*infinitely beyond our comprehension*." Pascal's fascination with the mathematically infinite, which proved helpful in his discussion of human disproportion (199/72), may here imply an impenetrable intellectual roadblock between humans and God. If we can know *nothing* about God, why should we suppose that such a God will reward those who believe in God? Maybe God would reward those who disbelieve in God!

Pascal's discussion of the logic of the hidden God turns on God being a personal Being who reveals himself to those who sincerely pursue him. But even the concept of personality cannot be applied to a God who *infinitely* transcends our understanding. No analogy between human persons and a divine person would then obtain. If so, Pascal's other crucial arguments—from anthropology, Scripture, etc.—would crumble, since an argument for the Christian God would be impossible.

Given the textual and literary problems of the wager fragment, it is fair to grant Pascal some charity—especially in light of the larger themes he states more clearly and plausibly elsewhere. I suggest the prologue was not meant to nail the door shut on divine knowledge. In fact, Pascal makes a positive claim in the prologue about God's moral character: "God's justice must be as vast as his mercy. Now his justice towards the damned is less vast and ought to be less startling to us than his mercy toward the elect." The force of the prologue may simply be that God's transcendence (indicated by "infinity") renders knowledge of the divine more obscure and less obvious than knowledge of other things. This chimes in with Pascal's argument on the "hiddenness of God." God may be hidden, but God may reveal himself as well (see chapter seven). The fact that there are no rational "proofs" for God does not rule out all knowledge of God. One may come to know something by other means than that of "proof."

The Wager Proper

Having been presented with the options of God's existence or non-existence in a situation where reason cannot decide the case either way by proofs, Pascal's interlocutor protests that no decision should be made. One should merely be agnostic and indifferent (Pyrrhonism).

Pascal responds that one *must* wager. Uncommitted agnosticism is not an option: "There is no choice, you are already committed. Which will you choose then?" Pascal does not elaborate on this, but his point should stand, with one qualification. With regard to the truth or error of two mutually exclusive propositions A and B, one can (1) believe A (and so disbelieve B) or (2) believe B (and so disbelieve A) or (3) suspend judgment about A and B. This is true for Pascal's interlocutor. He could remain uncommitted concerning theism. But the option becomes "forced," to use William James's term, when a prudential element is added.[4] We cannot avoid the issue by remaining skeptical because, "although we do avoid in that way error *if religion be untrue*, we lose the good, *if it be true*, just as certainly as if we positively chose to disbelieve."[5]

In other words, not to believe in theism, either as an unbeliever

77

or as an agnostic, means to forfeit the *benefits* promised only to the believer (eternal life), should theism be true. Deciding not to choose has the same result as choosing not to believe in God. In this sense, "you are already committed." In the final analysis, to be apathetic is to be antithetical. Our lease on earthly life is of limited duration, and we don't know when it will be up. Therefore, the decision should weigh heavily on us. In William James's words, such a choice is "momentous" and not "trivial" because the stakes are high, the opportunity is unique, and the choice is irreversible.[6] Pascal addresses his arguments to the Pyrrhonist, who would rather suspend judgment and cultivate ataraxia. What lends urgency to the situation, as Pascal mentions elsewhere, is that if one dies "without worshipping the true principle" (that is, the true God), one is forever lost (158/236). Proper *worship* is Pascal's concern, not mere theistic assent. God without Christ is mere deism (449/556).

Pascal next examines in detail the matter of prudential benefits and detriments. He exhorts the skeptic to seek truth in matters of ultimate concern, given the prudential possibilities, even if his chances of finding it through unaided reason alone appear dim. He says that "since a choice must be made," one should consider which option is most desirable. There are two things to lose: the true and the good. And there are two things to avoid: error and wretchedness. What is at stake is one's "reason and will" and one's "knowledge and happiness." Pascal then argues that since you must choose between atheism and theism, "your reason is no more affronted by choosing one than the other." Pascal seems to be assuming an intellectual standoff on the existence and nature of God. One might revise this point to say that since the reasons for unbelief are no better than the reasons for belief (at this stage of the game), and since Pascal's previous arguments have rendered Christianity at least credible, one's reason is not offended in further pursuing Christianity, especially if one could find further verification of its truth claims as a religious participant who has decided to wager.

Pascal then invokes the prospect of an eternal kind of perfect happiness. First, we should consider the gains and losses involved in betting that God exists. If we bet on God, and God exists, we win everything. If we bet on God and God does not exist, we lose nothing. Pascal then exhorts the interlocutor: "Do not hesitate, then; wager that he does exist." The interlocutor responds by wondering if he might be wagering too much. Pascal replies that since we *must* play the game and since there is an equal chance of winning or losing, risking one life for the chance of two or three lives would be worth the wager. But there is in this case an *eternity* of happiness to be won if God exists and one believes in God. Therefore, even if the chance of winning is less than one in two, but remains more than zero, a wager is advisable because of the chance of an infinite reward. In the God-wager, there is "an infinity of an infinitely happy life to be won, one chance of winning against a finite number of chances of losing, and what you are staking is finite." Pascal is not simply speaking of the quantity of happiness but of its quality as well. The beatific vision outshines infinitely any earthly allure.

> That leaves no choice; wherever there is infinity, and where there are not infinite chances of losing against that of winning, there is no room for hesitation, you must give everything. And thus, since you are obliged to play, you must be renouncing reason if you hoard your life rather than risk it for an infinite gain, just as likely to occur as a loss amounting to nothing.

Pascal subtly shifts the meaning of the word "reason" in this passage. Earlier he said that the existence of God could not be decided by reason; there are no conclusive theistic "proofs." Now he is claiming that one would be renouncing *reason* not to wager on God. In the former case, Pascal is referring to what could be called *theoretical* reason, or reason used as a tool to determine the rational status of propositions. In the latter case, Pascal uses reason in the sense of *prudential* reason, or reason as a means of calculating personal benefit or detriment. This distinction plays a vital role in the wager.

There is some controversy at this point whether the wager demands that the chance of God's existence be at least even or whether any nonzero chance will suffice to generate the wager. The answer is difficult to determine from the text. Some think that Pascal means that even if the odds for God's existence are very low, the positive reward of eternal life overwhelms the risk factor, and one should still wager on God. Pascal speaks of "one chance of winning against finite chances of losing" but at the end of the discussion he seems to imply that the bet is only worth it if the odds are even. Rather than debating interpretations, I suggest that what Pascal needs in order to ground the wager argument is the rough plausibility of what he has argued concerning the intellectual respectability of Christianity. Whatever the possible benefits for a belief may be, at some point (which is, admittedly, difficult to determine) one loses one's intellectual rectitude by attempting to believe something that is positively irrational on theoretical grounds simply because of some huge potential reward for so believing. However, as I note later, one's *intellectual* confidence in God may grow through a suitable spiritual experiment.

Pascal then considers the objection that one should not wager on God because the certainty of the finite reward of a worldly and enjoyable life outweighs the uncertainty of the infinite reward if God exists. He argues that a gambler is not sinning against prudential reason when he takes a certain finite risk in the hope of an uncertain finite gain, so long as the odds are even. "Thus our argument carries infinite weight, when the stakes are finite in a game where there are even chances of winning and losing and an infinite prize to be one."

Pascal concludes the section on the prudential reasons for belief in God with the strong statement that "this is conclusive and if men are capable of any truth this is it." The interlocutor agrees with Pascal but asks if there is "really no way of seeing what the cards are?" Pascal replies, "Yes. Scripture and the rest, etc." Pascal means the kinds of arguments he makes elsewhere in the *Pensées* about the historicity and authenticity of Christianity—the "proofs of religion." One may not be ready to consider earnestly these "proofs" until one can understand just what is at stake.

The interlocutor complains that although he is forced to wager given the prudential logic of the argument, he cannot believe. What can he do? Pascal recommends a kind of spiritual experiment. He argues that the interlocutor should realize that this unbelief is "because of your passions, since [prudential] reason impels you to believe and yet you cannot do so." The answer, then, is not to multiply proofs of God's existence, but to diminish one's passions, which counteract the clear command of prudential reason. The interlocutor should follow the example of those who once were in his skeptical shoes but who now wager all they have because they have been cured of the affliction of doubt. These souls "behaved as if they did believe, taking holy water, having masses said, and so on." Then the doubter will end up believing quite naturally and will become more "docile." The interlocutor objects that he is afraid of this, but Pascal consoles him by saying that he has nothing to lose and that this docility will diminish the passions that keep him from believing.

Pascal adds that if one wagers on God, one will become "faithful, honest, humble, grateful, full of good works, a sincere, true friend," although "noxious pleasures" of the flesh will be prohibited. The wagerer will find that he even benefits in this life by increasing in certainty to the point that the idea of risk becomes negligible, and "in the end you will realize that you have wagered on something certain and infinite for which you have paid nothing." This fills the interlocutor with delight. Pascal responds that his argument comes from a man who has beseeched the infinite and indivisible Being that the doubter might submit to God for his own good and for the glory of God. This coda ends the fragment. The argument was no game for Pascal.

Wagering: Risks and Rewards

Pascal says that one will "lose nothing" if one wagers on God and God does not exist. Yet one will lose *the truth* of the matter by wagering wrongly. According to one reading of the wager argument, the risk of losing truth is not a vital issue because the truth cannot be known by theoretical reason. If one must choose under *absolute* uncertainty, the loss of truth is simply a risk one must take either way one chooses. The issue of self-deception or intellectual impropriety never arises.

But according to my reconstruction, the loss of truth *is* a relevant consideration. This is because the wager itself can only be rational if it can be intellectually justified by Pascal's other arguments about the respectability of Christianity. (Absolute agnosticism stultifies any rational wagering.) Suppose one wagers on God incorrectly and persists in that wager. By being a theist when atheism (or some other nonChristian worldview) is the case, one loses the possibility of possessing the truth. There *is* an intellectual risk to be taken once the door is opened to the rational appraisal of the issues at stake. The same holds true for the atheist. He risks losing the truth should his position be false

If Christianity is true, the prudential benefits for believing (eternal life) far exceed those offered by believing in atheism (finite pleasures). The prudential detriments of not believing if Christianity is true (loss of eternal life) also far outweigh the detriments of not believing atheism if it is true (loss of finite pleasures). Pascal is right to affirm that eternal bliss outweighs any finite good and eternal loss is far worse than mere extinction.[7] But he is wrong in thinking that the theist really risks nothing. All the contestants risk the possibility of losing the truth if they wager wrongly.

If Many Gods, Why One Wager?

One of the most persistent criticisms of the wager argument is the "many gods objection." Critics attack Pascal for limiting the choices to atheism and Christianity when other worldviews, with other prudential outcomes, may be true. Does Pascal give sufficient reasons to wager on Christianity instead of other religions? Why wager on the biblical God and not Allah or Brahman or even the Great Pumpkin?

These criticisms hinge on the agnostic prologue to the wager argument in which Pascal is taken to be stating that reason can contribute nothing about the nature of an infinite. The number of possible deities with varying predilections for rewards and punishments is endless. One possible god could damn those who believe in him. Who knows what possibilities might obtain?

These criticisms are apt if we consider sheer logical possibilities over which theoretical reason is utterly impotent to adjudicate— although it seems strange to generate religious possibilities outside of the existing religions of the world. Pascal cuts the ground from under himself if he cannot stipulate that the God one is betting on is the kind who requires belief in him for salvation. The right sort of deity must be singled out of the metaphysical crowd. But if Pascal has argued elsewhere that the notion of the *Christian* God is at least plausible and attractive (12/187), then the wager, understood as a spiritual experiment, is warranted. If the concept of God is indeterminate, the prudential considerations cannot come into play because we do not know what we are betting on at all—something a gambler must know in order to make a prudentially rational wager in the first place.[8]

Yet if Pascal has shown that the idea of the Christian God is rationally plausible and prudentially compelling, what of other established religious traditions? In considering possible wagers, we need to consider religions that have reward and punishment systems similar to Christianity. The tradition most similar to Christianity seems to be Islam because it is monotheistic, claims to be based on a divine revelation, affirms the actuality of heaven and hell, and demands faith in Allah as necessary for salvation.

Pascal was well aware of Islam and other religions besides Christianity and Judaism. He argues that Mohammed was inferior to Christ as a religious leader, because, unlike Christ, Mohammed was neither foretold through prophecy nor did he himself prophesy (209/599). Jesus performed miracles; Mohammed did not. Pascal also claims that the Koran is less historically and logically credible than the

Bible; for example, he says that the Koran contains teachings that are clear, yet unbelievable and implausible, such as its doctrine of paradise. These ideas render its obscurities incredible as well. They should not be viewed as profound mysteries. Contrariwise,

> It is not the same with Scripture. I admit that there are obscurities as odd as those of Mahomet, but some things are admirably clear, with prophecies manifestly fulfilled. So it is not an even contest. We must not confuse and treat as equal things which are only alike in their obscurities, and not in the clarity which earns respect for the obscurities (218/598). [9]

Islam also lacks the crucial doctrine of original sin, which Pascal takes as having unique explanatory and apologetic force for Christianity (see chapter eight). Pascal in effect argues that Islam is evidentially inferior to Christianity ("it is not an even contest"), although the sum of his statements does not mount a sustained or thorough critique of Islam—a religion that would not have appealed to many of his French contemporaries. [10] His approach is to argue that some theologies are less credible than others, even if none can be *demonstrated* as true through theoretical reason alone. Pascal needs to give Christianity some evidential edge over any other heaven and hell oriented religion in order to justify the wager, at least according to my reconstruction of a plausible wager argument.

Other religions lacking the doctrines of heaven and hell may also offer prudential incentives, but they are less charged prudentially than Christianity and Islam. Both Hinduism and Buddhism teach the doctrine of reincarnation, wherein the postmortem state is not seen as necessarily eternal. Any number of lifetimes may be needed to neutralize bad karma and attain ultimate enlightenment, after which one escapes samsara (the wheel of rebirth) and need not reincarnate. According to Hinduism and Buddhism, if one wagers incorrectly—say on Islam or Christianity—in this life, a religious adjustment is available in another incarnation. But Christianity and Islam offer no such second (or millionth) chance. The stakes are higher and the time allotted to wager is far shorter—one life. Therefore, even if one finds the apologetic case for Hinduism or Buddhism plausible, given the prudential considerations of Christianity and Islam, one should attempt to rule out these high risk monotheistic faiths before pursuing Hinduism or Buddhism—unless, of course, one deems Hinduism or Buddhism so intellectually superior that one can find no rational interest in Christianity or Islam at all.

Even if other spiritual experiments were *conceivable*, this would not, in itself, seem to undermine the advisability of a Pascalian experiment if Pascal—or a Pascalian—were to establish its prudential and evidential warrant. If one becomes convinced through the spiritual experiment that one has sufficient reason, both epistemic and prudential, to believe in the hidden God as the true God, then further experiments would not be in order in light of Christianity's claims to religious sufficiency and uniqueness. Yet this does not mean that one could not choose to cease believing in Christianity. But as long as one believes, no other quests are appropriate because religious faith—more than the initial spiritual experiment—makes a total demand on a person.[11]

Is It Religious Brainwashing?

Pascal's language indicates that by engaging in certain religious activities, the wagerer will become "docile" (*abestira*) and eventually believe, as others have done. This method refers to the order of the body, or our mechanical nature. Pascal's approach to developing belief is open to the charge of self-inflicted religious brainwashing. Becoming habituated to the proposition "God exists" such that one believes it gives no rational justification for the belief. Nor does habituating oneself to the proposition "God does not exist" make that belief rational. Habituation is not argumentation. If the genesis of any belief is reducible to habituation alone that belief is not epistemically justified.

Pascal may not be arguing so crudely. He claims that the interlocutor's passions inhibit belief because prudential reason would otherwise impel him to believe. To become "docile" refers to the neutralizing of these inhibiting passions such that belief becomes possible. If so, this is not a case of brainwashing. It involves an element of testing, as Pascal says elsewhere in a dialogue:

> 'I should have given up a life of pleasure,' they say, 'if I had faith.' But I tell you: 'You would soon have faith if you gave up a life of pleasure. Now it is up to you to begin. If I could give you faith, I would. But I cannot, nor can I test the truth of what you say, but you can easily give up your pleasure and *test* whether I am telling the truth' (816/240; emphasis added).

84

As an Augustinian, Pascal believed that the person was essentially motivated either by concupiscence or charity—in other words, by one's fallen nature or by grace. If one is dominated by concupiscence, religious truth is unavailable. If one is willing to suspend or at least attenuate foul passions, charity may break through and faith ensue.

The Gospel of John reports Jesus saying to some unbelieving religious leaders, "How can you believe [in me] when you seek approval from others?" (John 5:44). He contends that prideful regard for status could keep one from seeing the truth. Along these lines, consider the case of a prideful actor named Charles who, now being past his prime, refuses to recognize the brilliance of a younger actor, Rodney, who is superbly executing the roles Charles once excelled in performing. But because of his age, Charles can no longer play the parts that once made him famous and which are now catapulting Rodney into fresh celebrity. The elder's pride and jealousy blinds him to the talents of his younger "rival." But Charles is counseled by a wise friend—who is interested in reconciling him to Rodney—to watch Rodney's best acting performances on video three times within one week. In so doing, the friend hopes that Charles's obtuseness will be overcome. Charles reluctantly agrees and later confesses Rodney's greatness, along with admitting the blindness of his former pride. Now he has eyes to see.

Pascal's recommendation of religious practices does not necessarily involve brainwashing, but rather a vulnerability to persuasion through various religious practices that may serve to temper the passions and thus open one to certain claims not otherwise convincing and to experiences not otherwise possible. This may, in fact, be what Pascal meant when he said that after wagering, "you will realize that you have wagered on something certain and infinite for which you have paid nothing" (418/233). "Certain" may entail an intellectual richness that exceeds what is possible through mere habituation.[12] Pascal elsewhere speaks of habituation or "custom" as helping to ground certain beliefs in a rational manner (821/252).

Is it True Faith?

Critics argue that wagering faith little resembles true religious faith for at least two reasons. First, one cannot be said to have faith if there is any tentativeness involved. The idea of testing a commitment with an experiment is inherently irreligious because religion demands absolute faith and commitment. Second, wagering faith is rejected because it is cultivated only to save one's own skin and get a heavenly payoff; it is merely mercenary.

First, Pascal's Christian tradition offers incentives for those not yet fully convinced to seek fuller assurance. Jesus advises that if his hearers ask, seek, and knock they will receive an answer (Matthew 7:7-8). When Jesus is confronted by a man who pleads, "I do believe, help me overcome my unbelief," he does not rebuke the man but responds to his imperfect faith and grants him his desire (Mark 9:14-29). Jesus also comments that faith as small as a mustard seed is sufficient for great things (Matthew 17:20).

Second, one who wagers on God need not be a religious mercenary who commits all intellectual and moral integrity to the flames for the off chance of infinite reward. As I see the wager, one need not transgress any intellectual or ethical standard by wagering on God. Self-interest, a normal human regard, need not be noxiously selfish. Jesus invoked self-interest, along with a comparison of finite and infinite goods, when he asked, "What good will it be for you to gain the whole world, yet forfeit your soul? Or what can you give in exchange for your soul?" (Matthew 16:25-26).

The wager can be seen as a first step in the process of possible belief development.[13] Because beliefs cannot be taken up at will, a process is undertaken which may result in full-fledged belief, if certain conditions obtain. Pascal himself is aware of the difference between true conversion and prudential exploration. The wager appeals to self-interest, but avoids brute selfishness if for no other reason than that the one wagering must begin to inhibit his worldly passions for the sake of religious participation. Pascal crisply articulates the meaning of robust faith as against leaner varieties:

> True conversion consists in self-annihilation before the universal being whom we have so often vexed and who is perfectly entitled to destroy us at any moment. . . . It consists in knowing that there is an irreconcilable opposition between God and us, and that without a mediator there can be no [salvation] (378/470).

Pascal says that the experimenter should act as if he believed by doing things like attending masses and taking holy water. This, he says, has helped many others with doubts. Pascal is within the Roman Catholic tradition, but the means at the disposal of the experimenter can be filled out a bit more ecumenically.

To act as if one believes means to engage in activities thought to build or strengthen faith. This could include involvement with religious services, the reading of Scripture and devotional materials, prayer and meditation, and association with believers on matters of spiritual concern. This kind of active participation need not be a case of uncritical engagement, but rather of sympathetic involvement. Ninian Smart has rightly observed that philosophers have tended to treat religious questions as merely metaphysical assertions in abstraction. Some sympathetic imagination and even participation is required to understand a religious claim in the holistic milieu in which it functions, even if this falls short of total commitment.[14]

Pascal emphasized both the cognitive and physical sides of spirituality:

> We must combine outward and inward to obtain anything from God; in other words, we must go down on our knees, pray with our lips, etc. . . . . If we expect help from this outward part we are superstitious, if we refuse to combine it with the inward part we are being arrogant (944/250).

The conclusion is that one may act "as if" one were a believer, but only if hypocrisy and self-deception are ruled out. Pascal certainly does not want to encourage self-deception: "Men often take their imagination for their heart, and often believe they are converted as soon as they start thinking of becoming converted" (975/275).

I suggest that the prudential factors raised by the wager are sufficient to generate a spiritual experiment, once the concept of God is rendered sufficiently intelligible to justify the rationality of such a venture. Therefore, a spiritual experiment—when properly conceived and executed—can be a fitting test for the paramount claims at issue.[15]

---

[1] Anthony Levi, "Introduction," in Blaise Pascal, *Pensées and Other Writings*, trans., Honor Levi; intro and notes by Anthony Levi (New York: Oxford University Press, 1995), viii.

[2] Alban Krailshaimer, *Pascal* (New York: Hill and Wang, 1980), 57.

[3] The idea of "infinite number" seems incoherent. For any number (even or odd) one can imagine a greater number. However, if Pascal means something like "numerical infinity" or the set of all numbers, the concept becomes (somewhat) more intelligible.

[4] See William Rowe, *Philosophy of Religion* (Belmont, California: Wadsworth Publishing Company, 1978), 178-180.

[5] William James, *The Will to Believe* (New York: Dover Publications, 1956), 26.

[6] Ibid., 3-4. We should amend James by noting that one may put off a religious decision or change one's religious beliefs before one's death. However, in biblical language, one may so "harden one's heart" that such a deathbed conversion becomes a psychological impossibility.

[7] Pascal does not overtly mention hell in the wager, but it seems implied; he endorses the doctrine of eternal punishment in *Pensées* (152/213), which emphasizes the fragility of life situated between heaven and hell.

[8] See Daniel Kolak, *In Search of God: The Language and Logic of Belief* (Belmont: Wadsworth Publishing Company, 1994), 150-151.

[9] See also 207/597; 209/599; 321/600. See chapter ten for discussion of Pascal's view of Christ's place in biblical prophecy.

[10] For a debate between a Muslim and a Christian apologist, see Josh McDowell and John Gilchrist, *The Islam Debate* (San Bernardino, CA: Here's Life Publishers, Inc., 1983).

[11] See Douglas Groothuis, "Obstinacy in Religious Belief," *Sophia* 32, no. 2 (July 1993): 25-35.

[12] See Douglas Groothuis, "Wagering Belief: Examining Two Objections to Pascal's Wager," *Religious Studies* 30 (1994): 479-86.

[13] See Nicholas Rescher, *Pascal's Wager: A Study of Practical Reasoning in Philosophical Theology* (Notre Dame, IN: University of Notre Dame Press, 1985), 117-133.

[14] Ninian Smart, *The Philosophy of Religion* (New York: Random House, 1970), 25.

[15] For more on the evidential value of a spiritual or devotional experiment, see Caroline F. Davis, *The Evidential Force of Religious Experience* (New York: Oxford University Press, 1989).

10

Christ, Spirituality, and the Meaning of Life

We complete our tour of Pascal by perusing a topic he took to be of preeminent importance: Jesus Christ and the meaning of life. That Pascal spoke so directly spoke to spiritual questions concerning the meaning of life in his philosophizing may be one key to his perennial appeal; it may also explain why he is excluded from many writings on the history of philosophy. He gives an overtly theological assessment of the meaning of life, which draws on his arguments concerning the nature of humanity, our knowledge of God, and religious experience.

"The meaning of life" usually means the significance of the universe and one's place in it—which encompasses the nature of humanity, its origin and destiny in cosmic scope. The meaning of life has of great interest to philosophers; yet, not a few modern philosophers have rejected the question as unanswerable or even unphilosophical. Thomas Nagel concludes *What Does it All Mean?* by addressing this. After rejecting any theistic meaning to life, he concludes that while it may "take the wind out of our sails," we should acknowledge that "life may be not only meaningless, but absurd."[1] Nagel does not develop the ethical, political, or psychological implications of such an approach (which suggest nihilism), but he believes a thinking and mature person must learn to live with the implications, whatever they may be.

Philosophers have offered many takes on the meaning of life, ranging from Stoicism's resignation to fate to nihilism's embrace of meaninglessness to existentialism's revolt against absurdity.[2] Pascal offers another answer. Life apart from God is absurd or "wretched," and one ought to be distressed over it; one ought not seek solace in diversions or be merely indifferent. We find meaning for life through recognizing our wretchedness (of being deposed royalty), seeking God for intellectually and existentially satisfying answers, and receiving the grace of God offered in the Mediator, Jesus Christ. Pascal supplies rational arguments for the Christian perspective on human nature and why the knowledge of God is obscure but not impossible ("the hidden God"). Although his answers are theologically-inspired and not derived from autonomous reason alone, he claims they do not conflict with reason and speak to the deepest human needs.

There is a Redeemer: Proved by Scripture

Pascal summarized the second part of his proposed *Apology* this way: "There is a Redeemer, proved by Scripture" (6/60). When the skeptical interlocutor in the wager asks if "there is really no way of seeing what the cards are," Pascal responds, "Yes. Scripture and the rest" (418/233). This material is in rougher shape than the fragments on the human condition. Nevertheless, some broad themes emerge.

> PROOFS—1. The Christian religion, by the fact of being established, by establishing itself so firmly and so gently, though so contrary to nature—2. The holiness, sublimity and humility of a Christian soul—3. The miracles of holy Scripture—4. Jesus Christ in particular—5. The apostles in particular—7. The Jewish people—8. Prophecies—9. Perpetuity: no religion enjoys [such] perpetuity—10. Doctrine, accounting for everything—11. The holiness of his law—12. By the order of the world (482/289).

Many fragments fill this out. One whole section of *Pensées* is devoted to miracles as evidence for faith.[3]

An argument Pascal values highly is often not considered today. He argues that many texts in the Hebrew Scriptures predict specific facts about the life of Christ, such as his place of birth, manner of ministry, and crucifixion (see 487/727). New Testament writers often view events in the Gospels as fulfilling Hebrew Scriptures written much earlier. If true, these facts would attest to both the supernatural character of the Hebrew Scripture (since so many "lucky guesses" are impossible) and to the divine authorization of Jesus himself as the promised Messiah. "The most weighty proofs of Jesus are the prophecies" (335/706). Jesus has a unique relationship to prophecy: "The prophets foretold events and were not foretold. Then came the saints, foretold but not foretelling. Christ both foretold and foretelling" (462/739). Pascal avers that Jesus is both prophetically foretold (by the Hebrew seers) and a prophet himself. He thus occupies a unique place. Contemporary Pascal scholars often overlook this argument, but it formed a central element of Pascal's overall approach to defending philosophically the Christian faith. [4]

Arguments from prophecy are often dismissed on the basis of an assumed anti-supernaturalism (or naturalism) that denies the possibility of divine communication in any form. Others say that such arguments do violence to the original meaning of the texts. If these objections can be overcome (which involves questioning naturalism's hegemony), a Pascalian sort of argument from prophecy is still possible. Not a few philosophically-inclined religious thinkers still employ it. [5]

Pascal reckoned that all of these twelve kinds of "proofs" mentioned above converged on Jesus (482/289). He is profoundly Christ-centered: "Jesus Christ is the object of all things, the centre toward which all things tend. Whoever knows him knows the reason for everything" (449/556).

Not only do we only know God through Jesus Christ, but we only know ourselves through Jesus Christ; we only know life and death through Jesus Christ. Apart from Jesus Christ we cannot know the meaning of our life or our death, of God or of ourselves. Thus without Scripture, whose only object is Christ, we know nothing and can see nothing but obscurity and confusion in the nature of God and in nature itself (417/548).

Pascal believed these pronouncements were warranted for many reasons. He does not merely assert a theological dogma without argument. He finds in Christ a matchless profundity of teaching that provides what we need to make sense of life. "Jesus said great things so simply that he seems not to have thought about them, and yet so clearly that it is obvious what he thought about them. Such clarity together with such simplicity is wonderful" (309/797). Pascal summarizes his understanding of Jesus' credentials.

He alone had to produce a great people, elect, holy and chosen, lead them, feed them, bring them into the place of rest and holiness, make them holy for God, make them the temple of

God, reconcile them to God, save them from God's anger, redeem them from the bondage of sin which visibly reigns in man, give laws to his people, write these laws in their hearts, offer himself to God for them, sacrifice himself for them, be a spotless sacrifice, and himself the sacrificer, having himself to offer up his body and blood, and yet offer up bread and wine to God (608/766).

Pascal also composed a short work summarizing and commenting on the life of Jesus as related in the Gospels. He arranged the materials chronologically into 354 statements taken from the Gospels, and supplemented by other biblical references and ideas from the church fathers and tradition. It came to be known as *The Compendium of the Life of Jesus Christ* (*Abrégé de la vie de Jésus-Christ*).

But the Gospels need not be taken on blind faith. Pascal appeals to internal evidence of their veracity with respect to the inclusion of elements unlikely in a work of religious fabrication (see 316/800). The Gospel writers "never [put] any invective against the executioners and enemies of Christ," which shows a "lack of affectation" (812/798). Pascal also argues against one common argument against the resurrection of Christ.

The hypothesis that the Apostles were knaves is quite absurd. Follow it out to the end and imagine these twelve men meeting after Jesus' death and conspiring to say that he had risen from the dead. This means attacking all the powers that be. The human heart is singularly susceptible to fickleness, to change, to promises, to bribery. One of them had only to deny this story under these inducements, or still more because of possible imprisonment, tortures and death, and they would all have been lost. Follow that out (310/801).

The argument that the apostles were deceived is equally implausible.

The apostles were either deceived or were deceivers. Either supposition is difficult, for it is not possible to imagine that a man has risen from the dead. While Jesus was with them he could sustain them, but afterwards, if he did not appear to them, who did make them act [as if Jesus were resurrected]? (322/802).

These fragments are not fully developed arguments, but suggestive notes. Nevertheless, Pascal believed that the case could be made, and his sense of spirituality and meaning in life in relation to Christ was rooted in his understanding of Jesus' resurrection as an historical fact with profound theological implications.[6] Modern scholars have recently debated this issue in sophisticated terms.[7]

Filling the God-Shaped Vacuum

In a different vein, Pascal argues that Jesus uniquely answers the profound needs of "deposed royalty," who cannot find adequate meaning and satisfaction in themselves or through worldly endeavors. Concerning "the God-shaped vacuum," Pascal explains:

> What else does this craving, and this helplessness, proclaim but that there was once in man a true happiness, of which all that now remains is the empty print and trace? This he tries in vain to fill with everything around him, seeking in things that are not there the help he cannot find in those that are, though none can help, since this infinite abyss can be filled only with an infinite and immutable object; in other words by God himself (148/428).

Pascal did not take this claim to be merely a post-dated check, cashable only in heavenly bliss (as much as this plays into the wager). A believer can experience something of spiritual renewal in this life (917/540). Several fragments present the rudiments of an argument for Christian theism based on religious experience. These augment Pascal's argument for Christianity from the human condition. He claims that Christians experience a dimension of life and a kind of spiritual awareness not available otherwise, and which is best accounted for on the basis of the divine influence mediated through the Incarnation.

> The Christian's God is a God who makes the soul aware that he is its sole good: that in him alone can it find peace; that only in loving him can it find joy: and who at the same time fills it with loathing for the obstacles which hold it back and prevent it from loving God with all its might (460/544; see also 352/526).

Pascal's "Memorial" is a specimen of his mystical encounter with God (913). However, his statements in *Pensées* on experiencing the reality of Christian life do not necessarily concern extraordinary mystical experiences, but focus on the spirituality of loving God and denying selfishness for the sake of something better (see 357/541).

Pascal finds in Christ a vital balance and a third way between presumption and despair. "Jesus is a God whom we can approach without pride and before whom we can humble ourselves without despair" (212/528; see also 351/537). In the same manner, Pascal argues briefly that the flourishing of Christianity against all manner of opposition—especially at its outset—attests to its supernatural origin and its unique ability to transform diverse people spiritually throughout history (433/783; 338/724).[8] It makes them both humble and confident.

Faith, Reason, and Argument

The humbling that Christianity teaches involves the submission of reason to divine revelation, that of the Bible and Christ himself. "Submission and use of reason; that is what makes true Christianity" (167/269). Yet Pascal takes this submission to be warranted and not irrational, given the credentials of Christianity's Scripture and its Savior. "The way of God, who disposes all things with gentleness, is to instill religion into our minds with reasoned arguments and into our hearts with grace" (172/185). Pascal argues that it is through the heart that we "know first principles, like space, time, motion, number," and that on such knowledge "reason has to depend and base all its argument" (110/282). A transformative knowledge of God, Pascal also claims, comes through the heart, but it is not unreasonable thereby.

> Those to whom God has given religious faith by moving their hearts are very fortunate, and feel quite legitimately convinced, but to those who do not have it we can only give such faith through reasoning, until God gives it by moving their heart, without which faith is only human and useless for salvation (110/282).

Although Pascal gives philosophical arguments for faith, he maintains that knowledge of God may sometimes be more intuitive than demonstrative. Pascal's worldview inspires him to produce apologetic arguments to persuade unbelievers, even if one may be within one's cognitive rights to believe without overt philosophical support (see 382/287).

In contemporary philosophical terms, Christian faith may be "properly basic"—intellectually justified for the believer apart from supportive arguments. A basic belief is not derived from some other more basic belief. Alvin Plantinga holds that Christian belief may be warranted without the aid of external evidence, in the same way that memory claims or our belief in the external world may be warranted without these beliefs needing any evidence outside of themselves for rational support. Not all basic beliefs are rational or "properly basic." (Belief in the Great Pumpkin would be an irrational basic belief.) Plantinga argues that Christian belief can be a properly basic belief, although he allows less room for positive evidence in defending Christian faith (beyond proper basicality) than does Pascal. [9]

Nevertheless, Plantinga's point is not too far from Pascal's famous aphorism, so often misunderstood: "The heart has its reasons of which reason knows nothing; we know this in countless ways" (423/277).

---

[1] Thomas Nagel, *What Does it All Mean?* (New York: Oxford University Press, 1987), 101.

[2] On several philosophical alternatives, both religious and nonreligious, see E. D. Kleme, ed. *The Meaning of Life* (Oxford University Press, 2000). The essay by William Lane Craig, "The Absurdity of Life Without God," 40-56, defends an essentially Pascalian perspective.

[3] Blaise Pascal, *Pensées*, ed. A. J. Krailsheimer (New York: Penguin Books, 1966), 281-306.

[4] See Jean Mesnard, *Pascal*, trans. and ed. Claude and Marcia Abraham (USA: University of Alabama Press, 1969), 73.

[5] See Thomas Morris, *Making Sense of it All: Pascal and the Meaning of Life* (Grand Rapids, MI: William B. Eerdmans Publishing Company, 1992), 162-168, and Norman Geisler, "Prophecy as Proof of the Bible," in *Baker Encyclopedia of Christian Apologetics* (Grand Rapids, MI: Baker Books, 1999), 609-617.

[6] See Morris, 173-176.

[7] See Paul Copan, ed., *Will the Real Jesus Please Stand Up? A Debate Between William Lane Craig and John Dominic Crosson* (Grand Rapids, MI: Baker Books, 1998).

[8] See Morris, 145-155. He calls this the "success argument."

[9] See also *Pensées* (380/284; 381/286), and Alvin Plantinga, *Warranted Christian Belief* (New York: Oxford University Press, 2000).

Bibliography

Adamson, Donald. *Blaise Pascal: Mathematician, Physicist, and Thinker About God.* New York: St. Martin's Press, 1995.

Allen, Diogenes. *Three Outsiders: Kierkegaard, Pascal, Weil.* Boston: Crowley Publications, 1983.

Bishop, Morris. *Pascal: The Life of Genius.* Westport, CN: Greenwood Press Publishers, 1968; original publication 1936.

Bishop, Morris. *Blaise Pascal.* New York: Dell Publishers Co., Inc., 1966.

Cailliet, Émile. *Pascal: The Emergence of Genius,* 2nd ed. New York: Harper and Brothers, 1961.

Coleman, Francis X.J., *Neither Angel Nor Beast: The Life and Work of Blaise Pascal.* New York: Routledge and Kegan Paul, 1986.

Jordon, Jeff, ed. *Gambling on God: Essays on Pascal's Wager.* Lanham, New York: Rowman and Littefield Publishers, Inc., 1994.

Kreeft, Peter. *Christianity for Modern Pagans: Pascal's Pensées Edited, Outlined, and Explained.* St. Louis: Ignatius Press, 1993.

Kolakowski, Leszek. *God Owes Us Nothing: A Brief Remark on Pascal's Religion and the Spirit of Jansenism.* Chicago: The University of Chicago Press, 1995.

Krailsheimer, Alban. *Pascal.* New York: Hill and Wang, 1980.

Mesnard, Jean. *Pascal.* Trans. Claude and Marcia Abraham. University of Alabama Press, 1969.

Morris, *Thomas. Making Sense of It All: Pascal and the Meaning of Life.* Grand Rapids, MI: William B. Eerdmans Publishing Company, 1992.

Mortimer, Ernest. *Blaise Pascal: The Life and Work of a Realist.* New York: Harper and Brothers, 1959.

O'Connell, Marvin R. *Blaise Pascal: Reasons of the Heart.* Grand Rapids, MI: William B. Eerdmans Publishing Company, 1997.

Pascal, Blaise. *Great Shorter Works of Pascal*. Trans. and intro. Émile Cailliet. Westport, CT: Greenwood Press Publishers, 1974.

Pascal, Blaise. *Oeuvres Complètes (l'Integrale)*. Louis Lafuma, ed. Paris: Editions du Seuil, 1963.

Pascal, Blaise. *Pensées*. Trans. A. J. Krailsheimer. New York: Penguin Books, 1966.

Pascal, Blaise. *Pensées and Other Writings*. Trans. Honor Levi. Ed. and notes by Anthony Levi. New York: Oxford University Press, 1995.

Pascal, Blaise. *Provincial Letters, Pensées, Scientific Treatises*. Great Books edition. Ed. Robert Maynard Hutchins. Chicago: Encyclopaedia Britannica, Inc., 1952.

Pascal, Blaise. *The Provincial Letters*. Trans. A. J. Krailsheimer. New York: Penguin Books, 1967.

Pascal, Blaise. *The Gospel of the Gospels: Abrégé de la vie de Jésus-Christ*. London: Umberto Allemmandi & Co., 1999.

Pascal, Blaise. *The Mind on Fire*. Ed. James Houston. Minneapolis, MN: Bethany Press, 1992.

Blaise Pascal. *Thoughts, Letters, Minor Works*. Ed. Charles W. Eliot. The Harvard Classics, vol. 48. New York: P.F. Collier and Son Company, 1910.

Patrick, Denzil, *Pascal and Kierkegaard: A Study in the Strategy of Evangelism*. 2 vols. London: Ludderworth Press, 1947.

Rogers, Ben, *Pascal*. New York: Routledge, 1999.

Rescher, Nicholas. *Pascal's Wager: A Study of Practical Reasoning in Philosophical Theology*. Notre Dame: University of Notre Dame Press, 1985.

Wells, Albert N. *Pascal's Recovery of Man's Wholeness*. Richmond, VA: John Knox Press, 1965.